THE CONFLICT MANAGEMENT SKILLS WORKSHOP

D1127532

THE CONFLICT MANAGEMENT SKILLS WORKSHOP

A Trainer's Guide

Bill Withers

AMACOM

American Management Association

New York • Atlanta • Brussels • Buenos Aires • Chicago • London • Mexico City
San Francisco • Shanghai • Tokyo • Toronto • Washington, D.C.

Special discounts on bulk quantities of AMACOM books are available to corporations, professional associations, and other organizations. For details, contact Special Sales Department, AMACOM, a division of American Management Association, 1601 Broadway, New York, NY 10019.
Tel.: 212-903-8316. Fax: 212-903-8083.
Web site: www.amacombooks.org

This publication is designed to provide accurate and authoritative information in regard to the subject matter covered. It is sold with the understanding that the publisher is not engaged in rendering legal, accounting, or other professional service. If legal advice or other expert assistance is required, the services of a competent professional person should be sought.

Library of Congress Cataloging-in-Publication Data

Withers, Bill.
    The conflict management skills workshop : a trainer's guide / Bill Withers.
       p. cm.
    Includes index.
    ISBN 0-8144-7092-0 (pbk.)
      1. Conflict management—Handbooks, manuals, etc. 2. Communication in management—Handbooks, manuals, etc. 3. Interpersonal communication—Handbooks, manuals, etc. 4. Employees—Training of—Problems, exercises, etc. I. Title.

HD42 .W58 2001
658.4'053—dc21

2001041215

Printing number

10 9 8 7 6 5 4 3 2 1

DEDICATION

For Julia and Mike, with thanks for years of love and support.

TABLE OF CONTENTS

PREFACE

Conflict happens.

People at work have plenty to disagree about: There is not enough stuff. There is not enough time. There is not enough money. There are not enough people. There is not enough space.

There are different ways of looking at things. There are different cultures. There are different needs. There are different plans. There are different views of ourselves, of the world, and where we fit into it all.

This book won't make conflict at work disappear, but you can use this book to help make conflict at work less threatening, easier to take, and maybe even a positive experience. The workshop that is outlined for you in this book is based on the idea that when you get a group of adults together to talk about conflict in a safe and thoughtful setting, you have made the first step toward defining what each individual—and the whole group—will decide to do to make conflict a positive force for themselves at work. Follow the steps in the workshop to help the group move from where they are to where they decide they need to be.

Helping new thinking to happen for one person or one group at a time can have a profound impact on your organization. As people think and talk about conflict at work, they begin to get a picture of what causes it and—more important—where they fit in the larger scheme of conflict where they work.

Read on to find out how to tap the expertise of the participants in your workshop group and to help them create a learning experience that can be their unique first step toward real change.

ACKNOWLEDGMENTS

This book would not have been written if my colleague Meloney Sallie-Dosunmu had not suggested it and introduced me to Jacquie Flynn, editor and navigator at AMACOM. Jacquie and her colleague Erika Spelman are great at what they do. They kept track of all the details and kept me on track. Of course, anyone who has been with me in workshops over the last several years has made a contribution. Without the adventure of learning and testing ideas together, nothing new would ever be created. Several friends and colleagues who train, write, and design had a hand in making sure that I presented the material in a way that others could use: Julia Hawrylo, Carrie Cox, Claudia Earley of Germaine Consulting, Dr. John McGlaughlin, Michele Remey Pepe, Karen Murdock, Kathi Keller, and Tamra Fleming. Julia, Karen, and John also helped as researchers. Keami D. Lewis played with the final versions of some exercises with me in workshop settings and made certain they truly were final. Dr. Jenny Beer is my thoughtful sounding board and "reality check." The action-planning exercise emerged from my work with Dr. Jay Rothman of the ARIA Group and from our many conversations. My employers and colleagues at R&B, Inc. were especially patient about sharing my focus as I worked on this book. Thanks to all.

THE CONFLICT MANAGEMENT SKILLS WORKSHOP

PART ONE

HOW TO LEAD THE CONFLICT MANAGEMENT SKILLS WORKSHOP

WHAT THIS BOOK IS ABOUT

This is a straightforward, easy-to-use book about helping people learn how to deal with conflict at work. The old story about the weather sometimes applies to conflict: Everybody talks about it, but nobody ever seems to do anything about it. Like the weather, conflict is merely there. Although some conflicts can be predicted, others often seem to well up out of nowhere. Still other conflicts seem to make sense to us only with the benefit of 20/20 hindsight. This book includes a number of simple ways to ensure that talking about conflict at work leads to people doing something about it.

The Conflict Management Skills Workshop provides trainers with a clear, step-by-step guide that is filled with exercises, discussion frameworks, and stories that I have developed over the years while working with groups of people in both business and nonprofit settings. The workshop approach is based on the understanding that any given group of adults has valuable experience that can be applied when learning about interpersonal skills. This book helps the facilitator to build a unique learning experience for any group by tapping into the group's unique background and collective wisdom.

We all have ideas, opinions, and experiences about conflict, but most of us have not had the opportunity to organize what we have learned into a theory that makes sense to us. This book gives facilitators and their groups the opportunity to organize their unique experiences into a plan that will work for their specific workplace. It teaches methods for helping a group's members to think about their experiences and to come to a unified conclusion about them.

You will then lead the people in your group into experiences that help them to test their theories so far. If their experiences do not match the theory, they can go back and tweak it a little or throw it out altogether. If the theory works most of the time, they can keep it and create theories that explain the exceptions.

A theory is handy because it saves us time when we are out experiencing by helping us to plan and predict, and to make sense of the world. Without a theory, each experience stands alone and we need to relearn and repeat mistakes. This book helps facilitators to get everybody's experiences on the table so that they can sift through these experiences and discover the patterns that will grow into a useful theory.

Sure, a trainer could look up theories and teach them to a class, but nothing will be remembered and used like a workable, homegrown rule of thumb. A theory is simply organized experience. It is a map of expectations that we draw after carefully thinking about where we have already been. We keep the map in our hip pockets to use when we encounter new situations that fit familiar patterns.

This book helps you as a facilitator to use your skill in creating a safe learning environment. You provide a safe place so that people can come to their own conclusions about what they need to learn to feel more successful when dealing with conflict at work. You will help people to rediscover the skills they have developed to work with conflict, and to sort them out from the practices that did not work.

Facilitators who lead groups through *The Conflict Management Skills Workshop* create a special opportunity for people to reflect on what has or has not worked for them in workplace conflict situations. The book starts with the basics before moving on to a powerful action-planning section that helps facilitators and their groups organize personal experiences into a map of expectations for what will work when going forward.

A BOOK FOR TRAINERS BY A TRAINER

This is a book for corporate trainers who need to lead a workshop in workplace conflict. *The Conflict Management Skills Workshop* is built around exercises, discussion questions, demonstrations, and stories distilled from my experiences leading workshops in various interpersonal skills over the years. The methods that work have been kept, and those that did not were left on the cutting-room floor. Although the book's focus is on conflict at work, there is a large amount of material that can be adapted for other interpersonal skills training. This material can help you tie your conflict workshop into what people in your company are learning about other topics such as communication, customer service, sales, cultural diversity, and leadership.

The Conflict Management Skills Workshop lends itself to every learning style. Activities allow for reflection, encourage interaction, allow for trial-and-error learning, and leverage the learner's relationship to others in the session. The session moves quickly from basic concepts to action planning, by using the participants' real-world experiences as the primary content. If you are an experienced facilitator, you may choose to borrow pieces from the book to strengthen the work that you are already doing. If you are less experienced or are looking for a detailed, proven plan for your workshop, then you can use the book as a step-by-step guide.

APPROACHING YOUR LEARNERS AS A ROOMFUL OF EXPERTS

When helping people learn interpersonal skills such as getting better at conflict, it is important to acknowledge the value of their experience. Trying to inoculate the group with what you think they need to know will not work. Whatever comes out of your mouth that runs counter to someone's experience or existing point of view will lead him or her to either openly disagree with you, resist participation, or turn you off altogether. These responses are not only classic trainer nightmares but can also severely limit the ability or willingness of the participants in your workshop to learn. If you spend the workshop using all your skill and energy to lead people to your preconceived conclusions, they will remember their resistance more than your content and there will be little positive behavioral change as a result of your time together.

The approach that I use to avoid this trap acknowledges that the best skill I can bring to a conflict skills workshop is my ability to create a safe place for learning. When you look at interpersonal skills training in this way, your energy as a facilitator is focused on the workshop's environment and structure rather than on trying to manage the responses of your learners.

It helps to think of the people attending the workshop as a roomful of experts on the topic. They may not realize it yet, but with your help, they can uncover a gold mine of experience, information, and points of view.

If you were asked to lead a symposium of world experts on the subject of conflict, you would:

- Thank them for coming, acknowledge their expertise, and respect what they have to say.

- Ask them questions that will help you test what you know about the subject.

- Make the symposium interesting to the experts. Challenge them to think, and create an environment in which they feel comfortable challenging one another's ideas.

- Capture their expertise by taking careful note of what they say and do.

- Ask the experts to create a statement about what they have learned from one another and what they intend to do next.

When you facilitate the workshop in this book, you will be in a room filled with people who have a wide variety of experience and ideas about conflict. They may not all feel particularly skilled in dealing with conflict, and they may never have been asked to organize their thoughts about it, but over the years each one of them has developed a set of conclusions about conflict.

They have theories of conflict and real-world experiences that have helped them create these theories. Therefore, in a very real sense, your workshop will be made up of a roomful of experts.

Your job as facilitator is to make it easy for these people to acknowledge their own and others' expertise. With your help, they will examine their conclusions, compare notes, and develop and scrutinize new theories.

Treat Them with Respect

You need to value the people in your workshop. No matter what you as the facilitator have read or heard or done about conflict, understand the power of the cumulative experience in your classroom.

Learn from Them

Your workshop should be an opportunity for the group to learn together. You have two main jobs here: one is to ask the questions that will help you learn from your experts, and the other is to enable your roomful of experts to ask the questions that will help them learn from one another.

You will lead your workshop in the manner of a person delegating a project to a group of able colleagues. They already know about conflict. You will give them a structure that will help them clarify and challenge what they know. As a successful delegator, you will give the group's members only as much as they need to complete the task, and you will trust them to work toward their goal. You will check in regularly and make certain that people feel safe asking for help as they go along.

Your roomful of experts need you to acknowledge their expertise. In most of their educational experiences and corporate training sessions, they have accepted the role of passive participant. You need to gently challenge them to acknowledge their own expertise and to use it. The exercises in your workshop begin with simple nonthreatening tasks and progress to riskier, more complex ones. The atmosphere of recognition and support that you help to create will increase the participants' comfort with risk and influence their willingness to learn.

Capture Their Expertise

Since you will be working with a roomful of experts, you will want to take note of what they are learning from each other. While you are together, many little lights will come on in people's heads. Some people may have breakthrough ideas for themselves, for you, for the group, or for the company.

These flashes may come at unexpected times. Some people need to talk about ideas, while others need to try them out. Some people need to read and think quietly, while others prefer sitting back, watching, and developing conclusions about what everybody else is doing.

When one of your experts comes up with a gem—rough or otherwise—be sure to note it. Slow the workshop down for a minute or two. Get off track. See what others think. Most important, use what you learn from each gathering of experts to make your next gathering even more powerful.

Report Their Findings

All that energy. All that learning. All the juice that is created when people get together and push against their own and one another's ideas. What a waste it would be if your workshop ended up as two pleasant days that had no lasting impact on the group or on the company.

As you work through this book, you will incorporate certain exercises and discard others. Whatever you do, use your workshop to create momentum for people to understand the value of conflict in their companies. Use the action plan in Handout 3.24: Action Plan, or create one of your own.

Training is a waste of time if what is learned is not set in motion back in the real world. Your knowledge of your company will tell you whether your planning will include systemwide change or whether the changes will be in individual thinking and behavior. Whatever the group's conclusion, help participants to find a way to reinforce their commitment to what they have learned to do.

The Conflict Management Skills Workshop will help you to create a positive experience for your roomful of experts. If this approach is new to you, follow the book closely the first time you facilitate the workshop. As you gain more feedback from your experts, let the workshop change to fit the people and the place where you work.

HOW THIS BOOK IS ORGANIZED: WHAT YOU WILL FIND INSIDE

This book is set up to provide everything you need to successfully facilitate *The Conflict Management Skills Workshop.* These introductory sections talk about the philosophy behind the book, tips on how you can best use the material to lead a successful workshop, descriptions of the various sections in the book, and workshop agendas.

The main body of the book includes the step-by-step Facilitator's Guide, containing detailed instructions for successfully conducting each of the workshop exercises, handouts, sample flip charts, and several brief stories that you can use to illustrate key points. A Participant Workbook contains reproducible handouts and stories, including reflection sheets, pre- and postevaluations, and action plans. In the Toolbox section, there is a list of other resources that can be found online or in your bookstore.

The Facilitator's Guide tells you what to say and when to say it. Special tips for trainers are included for additional clarification or to offer alternative activities. Stories that I have developed over the years are also included here. These brief examples will help you to quickly illustrate key ideas and to create a common set of reference points for the group. You can use the stories verbatim, adapt them to fit your specific situation, or use them to help you think of examples from your own experience.

The Conflict Management Skills Workshop moves quickly from one exercise to the next. The Facilitator's Guide provides detailed instructions and handouts specific to the exercises. Each exercise is outlined with its own set of objectives, a list of necessary materials, a detailed guide for conducting the exercise, and examples of any flip charts or handouts you may need. The handouts and stories recommended for the workshop are also included at the back of the book in the Participant Workbook.

The Participant Workbook can be used intact by the people in your workshop. If you are doing a shorter version of the workshop, you can excerpt the appropriate pages. Feel free to photocopy these pages.

The Toolbox section at the end of the book contains the outline for the full two-day workshop as well as recommendations for a one-day version and three half-day workshops that focus on specific skill areas. You will also find information about additional resources for gaining a background in approaches to conflict, systems thinking, and on facilitating this type of collaborative workshop.

In the section immediately following this one, Making This Book Your Own, there are detailed descriptions of each section of the workshop so that you can decide whether to pick and choose specific parts, use the entire workshop as is, or use the book as a springboard to create an original workshop of your own.

MAKING THIS BOOK YOUR OWN

If you use this book as a cookbook—a how-to for combining winning ingredients—you will facilitate a successful two-day workshop on conflict.

The more comfortable you are with the material in the book, the more flexible you will be. And the more flexible you are during the workshop, the more likely it is that you will connect with your workshop groups in the most meaningful way. So take the cookbook and make it your goal to learn it well enough so that you can work wonders without it.

Here is a good way to go about the job of making this your own book:

Before you lead your workshop, read the entire book. Several experienced trainers previewed *The Conflict Management Skills Workshop* and insisted that this first step is a must. As you read, write notes in the margins. Underline the parts that ring most true. Argue with the parts you disagree with. Change the book to fit what you know will be successful with the people you work with. Make notes, change the order of the exercises if it suits you, and try some new inventions of your own. Think of variations and invent new approaches.

Now, use your notes to create an outline that makes sense to you. Some trainers will end up with a one-page, six bullet–point outline and some handouts. Others prefer a word-for-word script. Most of us are somewhere in between.

Create a session or series of sessions that works for you and the people you will be serving. Please feel free to duplicate materials in the Participant Workbook for your sessions. As you work with this material, it will change and continually improve as long as you are as open to learning as you would want your participants to be.

Remember that the best cooks use cookbooks as a guide, then leave them behind to create their own masterpieces.

AGENDAS FOR *THE CONFLICT MANAGEMENT SKILLS WORKSHOP*

OUTLINE FOR FULL TWO-DAY WORKSHOP

Day One

9:00–9:10 Introduction to the Workshop (10 minutes)

Module 1. Awareness

9:10–9:15 Introduction and Objectives (5 minutes)

9:15–9:20 *The Bell Curve* (5 minutes)
This quick energizer opens the discussion about conflict and helps people to become comfortable with one another.

9:20–10:00 *Naming the Workshop* (40 minutes)
The workshop opens with an acknowledgment of the expertise in the room and a challenge to come to consensus on a name for conflict that works for everyone. Participants are introduced to classic consensus-building tools as they work on their first conflict together:

Brainstorming—The group generates multiple names for conflict.

- Discussion—The group presents arguments in favor of individual preferences.

- Voting—The group makes a "majority rules" decision and talks about how well it works as a conflict resolution tool.

- Building Consensus—The group is introduced to nominal group technique and applies it to the decision-making process.

10:00–10:15 Break

10:15–10:35 Ways of Seeing (20 minutes)
Story and Discussion
The facilitator and participants share stories and discussion about the idea that some conflicts are caused by the way people have learned to look at the world.

10:35–10:45 Ways of Knowing (10 minutes)
Truth—Some conflicts arise when people disagree on how to tell when something is true. The participants talk about what makes something ring true for them.

The Second Look—The facilitator tells stories about how changing the way we look at things may change our perception about what is worth fighting about.
The Farmer on the Porch—First impressions may not be enough.
The Pink Moment—There may be a benefit to looking in the opposite direction from everyone else.
The Colored Ball—The truth may change when we go over to the other side.
The Blind Men and the Elephant—The classic Sufi tale is retold and discussed.

10:45–11:00   Ways of Learning (15 minutes)
Losing Sara—This case study gives the group the opportunity to examine how different learning styles can contribute to workplace conflict.

11:00–11:15   Break

11:15–11:40   Ways of Living (25 minutes)
Do the Right Thing—A simulated culture exercise, *Do the Right Thing* gives participants the chance to be well-meaning yet misunderstood by someone with different customs. The discussion centers around how we take our customs for granted and how this can become fuel for conflict.

11:40–12:30   Ways of Seeing Conflict (50 minutes)
Sometimes the way we view conflict can contribute to how well we deal with it. Other times, differing views about conflict can cause more trouble than what we were fighting about in the first place.
Win, Lose, or Draw—One way of looking at conflict is as a contest to be won or lost.

Make It Even, Make It Bigger, or Make It Different

- Make It Even—Working through conflict by dividing things up
- Make It Bigger—Working through conflict by getting more of whatever needs to be shared
- Make It Different—Finding more than one way to work through a conflict by looking at what is being fought over in a new way

The Shared Resource
  Splitting "even-steven."
My Dad and the Last Brownie
  When people own the problem, they own the solution.

Two Sisters, One Orange
> Participants read a story about an innovative conflict approach and discuss questions to help them come to their own conclusions.

Reflection: *What Do I Think About Conflict Right Now?*
> The first of four Reflection Sheets. Your group stops for a moment to think and write privately about what they have learned so far.

12:30–1:30   Lunch

Module 2. Response

Participants examine the way they tend to respond to conflict and compare notes about what works best.

1:30–1:40   Introduction and Objectives (10 minutes)

1:40–2:20   Reflection: *"Good" Conflict?* (40 minutes)
> The group stops for a moment to think and write privately about whether conflict can be a positive force. They then join in a discussion about what elements lend themselves to positive conflict.

2:20–2:35   Break

2:35–3:35   *Party Time* (1 hour)
> An energetic exercise that helps participants come to some conclusions about whether there is one best way to respond to conflict.

3:35–3:50   Break

3:50–4:05   Reflection: *How Can This Possibly Be Good for Me?* (15 minutes)
> Another private reflection sheet that gives individuals a chance to think about whether they have come to any new conclusions about conflict.

4:05–4:20   Wrap Up Day One (15 minutes)

Day Two

9:00–9:10   Review of Day One (10 minutes)

Module 3. Actions

9:10–9:15   Introduction and Objectives (5 minutes)
Group members have made some decisions about conflict theory and now have a chance to plan actions for themselves going forward.

9:15–9:25	Conflict Intervention (10 minutes) Participants take a look at different ways to help other people work through conflict.
	Solving Problems—One way to help people is to guide them while they generate creative solutions to their problems.
9:25–9:30	Introduction (5 minutes)
9:30–9:35	*Two Siblings and One Orange, Take One* (5 minutes)
9:35–12:30	Practice Mediation (2 hours, 55 minutes) *Looking Neutral*—Food for thought about a key skill for helping other people in conflict.
12:30–1:30	Lunch
1:30–1:40	Introduction (10 minutes) **Transformation**—Another way to help people is to encourage them to learn about one another, themselves, and the ability they have to work through conflict together.
1:40–1:45	*Two Siblings and One Orange, Take Two* (5 minutes)
1:45–2:15	How Deep Is Too Deep? (30 minutes) The group talks about its comfort level when it comes to helping with other people's business.
2:15–2:30	Break
	My Personal Conflict Strategy—Participants work on developing their own conclusions about what to do about conflict at work.
2:30–2:31	Introduction (1 minute)
2:31–3:15	Choosing Thoughts (44 minutes)
3:15–3:30	Choosing Words (15 minutes)
3:30–3:45	Break
3:45–4:20	Choosing Actions (35 minutes)
4:20–4:35	Break
4:35–5:05	Our Group Conflict Strategy (30 minutes) Group members use this action-planning exercise to decide how they can work together to effectively deal with conflict at work.
5:05–5:20	Close (15 minutes) Check-in: Does our name for conflict still work? Individual objectives check Evaluation

OUTLINE FOR ONE-DAY WORKSHOP

If you only have one day to spend with your group, you can shorten the full workshop by omitting group approaches to conflict and focusing on interpersonal conflicts instead.

8:00–8:05	Introduction (5 minutes)
8:05–8:10	*The Bell Curve* (5 minutes)

8:10–8:30	Ways of Seeing (20 minutes)
	  Introduction
	  Story and Discussion

8:30–8:40	Ways of Knowing (10 minutes)
	  Truth
	  The Second Look
	  The Blind Men and the Elephant

8:40–8:55	Ways of Learning (15 minutes) *Losing Sara*
8:55–9:20	Ways of Living (25 minutes) *Do the Right Thing*

9:20–10:10	Ways of Seeing Conflict (50 minutes)
	  Win, Lose, or Draw
	  Make It Even, Make It Bigger, or Make It Different
	    Make It Even
	    Make It Bigger
	    Make It Different
	  Two Sisters, One Orange
	  Reflection: *What Do I Think About Conflict Right Now?*

10:10–10:25	Break

Response

10:25–11:00	Reflection: *"Good" Conflict?* (35 minutes)
11:00–11:10	Conflict Intervention (10 minutes)
11:10–11:15	*Two Siblings and One Orange, Take One* (5 minutes)
11:15–12:15	Lunch
12:15–3:00	Practice Mediation (2 hours, 45 minutes) *Looking Neutral*
3:00–3:15	Break
3:15–3:20	*Two Siblings and One Orange, Take Two* (5 minutes)

My Personal Conflict Strategy

3:20–3:21	Introduction (1 minute)
3:21–4:00	Choosing Thoughts (39 minutes)
4:00–4:15	Choosing Words (15 minutes)
4:15–4:45	Choosing Actions (30 minutes)
4:45–4:55	Close (10 minutes)

OUTLINE FOR HALF-DAY WORKSHOP: MEDIATION PRACTICE

This workshop stresses mediation skills. It is most effective with a small group of no more than ten people so that each participant gets at least two opportunities to practice mediating.

8:00–8:05	Introduction (5 minutes)
8:05–8:10	*The Bell Curve* (5 minutes)
8:10–9:00	Ways of Seeing Conflict (50 minutes)
	Win, Lose, or Draw
	Make It Even, Make It Bigger, or Make It Different
	Make It Even
	Make It Bigger
	Make It Different
	Two Sisters, One Orange
	Reflection: *What Do I Think About Conflict Right Now?*
9:00–9:05	*Two Siblings and One Orange, Take One* (5 minutes)
9:05–12:00	Practice Mediation (2 hours, 55 minutes)
	Looking Neutral
12:00–12:15	Break
12:15–12:20	*Two Siblings and One Orange, Take Two* (5 minutes)
12:20–12:30	Close (10 minutes)

OUTLINE FOR HALF-DAY WORKSHOP: CONFLICT AWARENESS

The first half of Day One in the Two-Day Workshop can stand alone to help people begin to examine their points of view about conflict.

9:00–9:05	Introduction and Objectives (5 minutes)
9:05–9:10	*The Bell Curve* (5 minutes)
9:10–9:50	*Naming the Workshop* (40 minutes)
	Brainstorming
	Discussion
	Voting
	Building Consensus
9:50–10:10	Ways of Seeing (20 minutes)
	Introduction
	Story and Discussion
10:10–10:25	Break
10:25–10:35	Ways of Knowing (10 minutes)
	Truth
	The Second Look
	The Blind Men and the Elephant
10:35–10:50	Ways of Learning (15 minutes)
	Losing Sara
10:50–11:05	Break
11:05–11:30	Ways of Living (25 minutes)
	Do the Right Thing
11:30–12:20	Ways of Seeing Conflict (50 minutes)
	Win, Lose, or Draw
	Make It Even, Make It Bigger, or Make It Different
	Make It Even
	Make It Bigger
	Make It Different
	Two Sisters, One Orange
	Reflection: *What Do I Think About Conflict Right Now?*
12:20–12:30	Close (10 minutes)

OUTLINE FOR HALF-DAY WORKSHOP: RESPONSES TO CONFLICT

The Response section of the workshop can stand alone as a half-day session. The emphasis is on making choices about how to respond in conflict situations. Whether they feel they give in too easily or react too strongly to conflict, this shorter workshop is helpful for individuals and groups who are not satisfied with the way they behave in conflict situations.

8:00–8:05	Introduction (5 minutes)
8:05–8:10	*The Bell Curve* (5 minutes)

8:10–8:30	Ways of Seeing (20 minutes)
	    Introduction
	    Story and Discussion

8:30–8:40	Ways of Knowing (10 minutes)
	    Truth
	    The Second Look
	    The Blind Men and the Elephant

8:40–9:05	Ways of Living (25 minutes) *Do the Right Thing*

9:05–9:55	Ways of Seeing Conflict (50 minutes)
	    Win, Lose, or Draw
	    Make It Even, Make It Bigger, or Make It Different
	        Make It Even
	        Make It Bigger
	        Make It Different

9:55–10:10	Break
10:10–10:50	Reflection: *"Good" Conflict?* (40 minutes)
10:50–10:55	Reflection: *How Can This Possibly Be Good for Me?* (5 minutes)

My Personal Conflict Strategy

10:55–10:56	Introduction (1 minute)
10:56–11:40	Choosing Thoughts (44 minutes)
11:40–11:55	Choosing Words (15 minutes)
11:55–12:20	Choosing Actions (35 minutes)
12:20–12:30	Close (10 minutes)

GETTING READY

The Preworkshop Questionnaire

This optional questionnaire can be sent out in advance of the workshop to help you get a feel for the group. It is a great way to encourage participants to think about conflict and the role it plays at work before they come to your session. More important, it gives the people who have signed up to work with you an idea of the types of things they will be thinking and talking about in class.

It is best to send out a memo along with the questionnaire that includes details such as start time and location about two weeks before the workshop. This gives people time to respond, and is near enough to your session date to serve as a mental warm-up. The memo and questionnaire can be found in Handouts I.1 and I.2.

You can refer to the general results of the questionnaire when processing the *Bell Curve* exercise (which you will see in the introductory part of the workshop).

The Ideal Room Setup

The ideal room setup should include the following items:

- Two or more easels with flip charts and markers
- Participant Workbooks that are preset at each seat
- Round tables that seat from four to six people

Use whatever furniture and space you have to set up a room that will support good conversations. If you do not have round tables, pull desks into a circle or arrange long tables into a horseshoe shape. People can line the inside and outside of the horseshoe for discussions across the table, sit along the outer side while you speak from the center, and use the empty inside of the *U* as a space for exercises and demonstrations. Participants will need a writing surface of some kind, so avoid providing only chairs.

If you are forced to use a massive conference table or some other formal setup that you cannot change, you should add touches that deformalize the atmosphere. Check whether casual clothing will be allowed. If there is space at one end of the room, set up some extra chairs as a conversation pit.

 TRAINER Tip: A good way to let people know that this will be a different experience from their typical business meetings is to add color and music to the setting. I have often photocopied the Participant Workbooks with different colored covers and spread them randomly on the table or tables. Some people will come in and take the seat that has the book with their favorite color. Others will try to analyze a pattern and choose a color based on what they think is some plan that you have. Still others will try to trade books to get the colors that they want. It starts the day off with people thinking, talking, and laughing.

I often have music playing in the room as people enter. If someone comes early, I ask that person to choose what music to play as people come in. Note: Some trainers like to use music during reading, writing, or reflection exercises. If you try this, ask the group how they liked it. Some people find it helpful. Others find it annoying.

GETTING YOURSELF READY

Remember that *The Conflict Management Skills Workshop* is most successful when you are relaxed and willing to let the group make its own decisions about what to dwell on. The first couple of times you lead the workshop you may want to stick close to the script, but as you become more comfortable with the material you can go with the flow and let the group spend time on the sections that are the most helpful. No matter how much you may know about the topic of conflict, it is important to remember that this group is more expert than you are when it comes to the participants' own conflicts and points of view.

Take a deep breath, let it out, and remove your trainer's hat. This can be difficult, especially when you use a different style in other training classes. It is not unusual for me to switch from something cut-and-dried, such as teaching OSHA regulations, to facilitating a participant-centered workshop on conflict. To help ensure that I successfully make the shift, I sometimes reread "Approaching Your Learners as a Roomful of Experts" in Part I before facilitating this type of workshop, or I talk through what I will be doing with another trainer.

Come to the workshop early so that you can greet people as they enter, check that everything is in place, and let yourself become excited about what you are going to learn along with your group.

 TRAINER Tip: A word about overheads, videos, and posters. I use these tools in many of my training sessions. They work fine, especially for a large group that stretches too far away from me to read my flip-chart scrawl. Overheads, videos, and posters focus the learner's attention on the specific information and conclusions that the teacher wants them to see at a specific moment in the training. They help trainers to control the order that information is presented in and to lead learners to the expected conclusion. We also use them to look good—they reinforce our professional expertise as trainers. However, I do not use overheads, videos, or posters for *The Conflict Management Skills Workshop.* Remember that the point of this workshop is to help people discover what they and their colearners know, adding to it through practice and refining it into some workable form that will help them in real life at work. Overheads, videos, and posters can be valuable training tools for other courses, but they can weaken a workshop designed to run off the power of the group's knowledge. These tools send the message that you have knowledge that the group does not have and that they should behave themselves and soak it up. Instead of using prepared peripherals, post your flip-charts around the room as you go. By the end of the workshop, the space will be filled with colorful representations of your group's ideas. In *The Conflict Management Skills Workshop,* you create a space for the exchange of ideas and help the people you are leading to fill it.

PREWORKSHOP MEMO

Date:

To:

From:

Re: *Conflict Management Skills Workshop*

Welcome to the *Conflict Management Skills Workshop.* This exciting two-day session will give us the opportunity to examine our current approaches to conflict, and decide how to change them if we need to.

We will be looking at where our ideas about conflict come from, how we feel about conflict at work, and how we think we can improve.

As a group, we will decide what we can do to make conflict at work a constructive force here at our company.

Please take a few minutes to fill out this questionnaire and return it anonymously to _____ no later than _____. Your responses will help us prepare for a workshop that best serves the needs of the group.

I look forward to seeing you on _____ at _____. We have a great deal of work to do, so please be prompt.

Thank you for your assistance.

PREWORKSHOP QUESTIONNAIRE

Please answer this quick questionnaire and return it to _____ by _____. Your answers will help us ensure that the workshop is a practical tool that is specific to your needs.

5 = Strongly Agree; 4 = Agree; 3 = Disagree; 2 = Strongly Disagree; 1 = Don't Know

1. I am good at handling conflict at work.　　　　　　5　4　3　2　1

2. I would rather avoid conflict than meet it head-on.　　　　　　5　4　3　2　1

3. I think what is right is worth fighting for.　　　　5　4　3　2　1

4. Some things are not worth fighting about.　　　　5　4　3　2　1

5. Only fight when you know you are going to win.　5　4　3　2　1

6. If I disagree with people at work, I will never get them to do the things that are important to me.　　　　　　5　4　3　2　1

7. I think we handle differences effectively here at our company.　　　　　　5　4　3　2　1

8. I am happy with the way that I deal with daily conflict.　　　　　　5　4　3　2　1

9. What causes conflict among people who work together at our company?

   _____

   _____

   _____

   _____

10. I think that our company is

    ❏ More able than　　❏ About the same as　　❏ Less able than

    other companies when it comes to dealing effectively with conflict.

11. I think that I am

    ❏ More able than　　❏ About the same as　　❏ Less able than

    other people when it comes to dealing effectively with conflict.

21

PART TWO

FACILITATOR'S GUIDE

Introduction to the Workshop

Commentary: Introduce yourself and review the workshop agenda.

 Facilitator: You may want to include a copy of your workshop agenda at the beginning of the Participant Workbook. If so, refer the participants to the agenda in their workbooks now. In addition, you should now refer participants to Handout II.1: Workshop Objectives.

Commentary: Welcome to your *Conflict Management Skills Workshop.*

Look around at all of the other people who are in the workshop with you. No two of us have had all of the same experiences. Everyone in the workshop, including you, has come to some conclusion about conflict. Some people think conflict is a good thing. Some think it should be avoided at all costs.

We each have a point of view about conflict that comes from what has or has not worked for us and from our beliefs about how we should live our lives. Everyone in the workshop is a philosopher. All of us have theories about conflict and what to do with it.

OBJECTIVES

Following are a few objectives to think about as you begin the workshop. During the two days of this workshop:

- You will have the opportunity to think about your point of view on conflict.

- You will have the opportunity to compare notes with the other people in the workshop.

- You will be able to test your point of view.

- You will have the opportunity to change your mind and influence others.

- You will have the opportunity to come to some agreement with your coworkers about ways to think about and respond to conflict at work.

- You will have a chance to remember what you already know about conflict, learn from others, and arrange all these ideas into your own practical theory.

- You will have a chance to join problem-solving sessions, speak up with new ideas, and learn about other people's points of view.

- You should be able to make decisions about how you will handle conflict as an individual and as part of this group.

👤 👤 👤 Group Activity: *Introductions*

Commentary: Ask the workshop's participants to introduce themselves and to tell you one thing they would like to get out of the next two days. Write each person's name and his or her personal objective on a flip chart and post it.

Tell the group that you will revisit their personal objectives during the workshop to ensure that they are being well-served.

WORKSHOP OBJECTIVES

INTRODUCTION

Welcome to your *Conflict Management Skills Workshop.* Look around at all of the other people who are in the workshop with you. No two of us have had all of the same experiences. Everyone in the workshop, including you, has come to some conclusion about conflict. Some people think conflict is a good thing. Some think it should be avoided at all costs.

We each have a point of view about conflict that comes from what has or has not worked for us and from our beliefs about how we should live our lives. Everyone in the workshop is a philosopher. All of us have theories about conflict and what to do with it.

OBJECTIVES

- During the two days of this workshop, you will have the opportunity to think about your point of view on conflict.

- You will have the opportunity to compare notes with the other people in the workshop.

- You will be able to test your point of view.

- You will have the opportunity to change your mind and influence others.

- You will have the opportunity to come to some agreement with your coworkers about ways to think about and respond to conflict at work.

- You will have a chance to remember what you already know about conflict, learn from others, and arrange all these ideas into your own practical theory.

- You will have a chance to join problem-solving sessions, speak up with new ideas, and learn about other people's points of view.

- You should be able to make decisions about how you will handle conflict as an individual and as part of this group.

Awareness

INTRODUCTION AND OBJECTIVES

Commentary: It is time to compare notes with other people in the workshop.

There is a saying that fish never talk about the water. What this means is that when we are involved in something every day or see something every day, we stop noticing it. We respond to it as if it is simply the way things are—or the way things must be.

Our relationship with conflict is similar. In this module, we examine the points of view that each one of us has developed about conflict over the years. There may be some surprises. Sometimes what we think about conflict and how we deal with it have become so automatic that we take these methods for granted. Most of us rarely take the time to think about conflict or to evaluate whether what we have figured out about conflict is working as well as we would like.

 Facilitator: Refer participants to Handout 1.1: Module 1 Objectives.

MODULE 1 OBJECTIVES

INTRODUCTION

It is time to compare notes with other people in the workshop.

There is a saying that fish never talk about the water. What this means is that when we are involved in something every day or see something every day, we stop noticing it. We respond to it as if it is simply the way things are—or the way things must be.

Our relationship with conflict is similar. In this module, we examine the points of view that each one of us has developed about conflict over the years. There may be some surprises. Sometimes what we think about conflict and how we deal with it have become so automatic that we take these methods for granted. Most of us rarely take the time to think about conflict or to evaluate whether what we have figured out about conflict is working as well as we would like.

OBJECTIVES

- As we open the session, you will begin deciding on the direction of the workshop that works best for you.
- We will work together to find the best name for conflict at our company.
- We will learn what other people think about conflict and compare it with our own points of view.
- You will have the opportunity to think about any new ideas that you would like to consider.

Commentary: Now quickly review the objectives for Module 1.

OBJECTIVES FOR MODULE 1

Following are some objectives to think about as you begin Module 1:

- In this module, you will begin deciding the direction of the workshop that works best for you.
- We will work together to find the best name for conflict at our company.
- We will learn what other people think about conflict and compare it with our own points of view.
- You will have the opportunity to think about any new ideas that you would like to consider.

 **Group Activity: *The Bell Curve***

Type
Icebreaker

Purpose
Set a tone of participation, give the facilitator and participants a quick check of participants' readiness and attitudes.

Equipment Needed
None

Preparation
None

Time
5 minutes

Commentary: Indicate two points along the wall or on the floor. Tell participants that one point represents, "I love conflict! I think it keeps the company going forward. Can't get enough of it!" The other point represents, "Eeek! Conflict! There is nothing worse for the company or for me. Get it out of my face!"

 Trainer Tip: If your training room is small, you may need to go out into a hallway for this exercise. As people line up according to their levels of comfort, be sure that they know that they can bunch up at whatever point they feel most comfortable.

People usually line up in a rough bell curve. You do not need to comment at this point; merely let everyone see where they are in relation to everyone else and where other people ended up. Then tell them it is time to line up again. This time one end represents, "I know everything there is to know about conflict," while the other end is, "I am clueless when it comes to conflict."

Let participants line up and make whatever comments or have whatever sidebar conversations that naturally emerge. Listen to them but do not comment. The exercise is best when it helps people to relax so that they begin talking to one another.

Debriefing

Wrap things up by commenting that the main benefits of the exercise are that it gets people accustomed to getting out of their chairs, moving around, and talking to one another and that it gives everyone a general idea of where the group stands on the general topic of conflict at work.

Tell the group that the next two days will be shaped in large part by their ideas and participation. Thank them, and ask them to return to their seats.

Option: If you used the preworkshop questionnaire, you can share the findings from the questions and compare them with what was shown in the lineup.

👤👤👤 Group Activity: *Naming the Workshop*

Type
Brainstorm

Purpose
This exercise lends itself to the early coming together of the group. As they begin to decide how they will talk about conflict, people discover a sense of ownership and begin to feel comfortable in the role of participant rather than merely being a recipient of the trainer's knowledge and opinions.

Equipment Needed
- Flip Chart 1.1: The Conflict Management Skills Workshop
- Markers
- Paper
- Pencils or pens
- Adhesive dots in a variety of colors

Preparation
- Make a copy of Flip Chart 1.1: The Conflict Management Skills Workshop.
- Check that each participant has paper and a pen or pencil.

Time
40 minutes

The Conflict Management Skills Workshop

Commentary: State that "conflict" is not the usual name we use when we are talking about conflict. Give a couple of examples of everyday names for conflict, such as:

- Row
- Squabble
- Fight
- Spat
- Quarrel
- Dispute
- Fracas
- War
- Rumble

Brainstorming

Instructions
Tell participants that the terms used for conflict vary widely. Ask them to take out a piece of paper and list as many terms for conflict as they can think of in three minutes.

Debriefing
When everyone has finished writing, ask each person to give you one name for conflict from his or her list.

Explain that you will keep going around the room until everyone's list is exhausted: "If someone else says a name for conflict that is on your list, cross it off and give me the next one that is on your list. If you think of more names as we go around the room, add them to your list. Once you run out of names for conflict, you can just say 'I pass,' when I come to you."

As participants tell you their names for conflict, write them on a flip chart.

 Facilitator: Once you have a complete list on your flip chart, read it back to the group.

 **Discussion**

Instructions

1. Ask participants to tell you whether there is a name for conflict that they do not understand or that they have a question about.
2. Ask the others in the group for an explanation.

TRAINER TIP: Be sure that your questions or comments about participants' names for conflict are respectful—people can be very attached to the words that they choose for expressing things that are important to them.

Tell the group that conflict is a topic that we all know something about. With your help as a facilitator, the people in the group will share what they know with one another and perhaps even reach an agreement about what conflict is and how to make it a positive force in your organization.

Voting

 Facilitator: Now vote for the best name for conflict. Distribute colored dots.

Instructions
Ask participants to stick a dot next to each of their three favorite choices on the posted flip chart. The name for conflict with the most dots wins. This voting method is more anonymous than a simple show of hands—and it gets people on their feet, moving and chatting with one another while they think.

Debriefing
When the number one name has been selected, ask whether anyone feels strongly about one of the names for conflict that was not chosen. Pay particular attention to words in languages other than English, unusual words, or words from a minority culture that were not chosen. Invite everyone to join in this discussion. Be aware when voting that majority rule is often a catalyst for conflict instead of a solution. Talk about that scenario.

Building Consensus

Commentary: Voting creates winners and losers. Tell participants that the majority wants to call conflict by the number one choice, but that you are going to attempt to reach consensus.

Instructions
Go around the room again, this time asking each person to vote out loud either yes, no, or pass for the number one word for conflict. If everyone votes yes on one name for conflict, it will be the term used for conflict for the remainder of the workshop.

Once everyone has voted on a specific name, ask for comments from anyone who voted no or pass. Allow the no or pass voters to persuade others or to be persuaded. When the discussion on a particular name for conflict is completed, go around the room again and ask for yes, no, or pass votes. Allow more discussion, and then vote again. If two rounds do not get consensus, move on to the next word. If you get a word that everyone votes yes on, it will be the name for conflict that you use for the remainder of the workshop.

If intonation or body language indicates to you that someone is not happy with his or her vote (for example, if you think that someone is going along because he or she feels pressured by the group), draw the person out. If someone wants to make a case for a word other than the number one choice, let him or her do so. Vote yes, no, or pass on this person's suggestion.

Debriefing

If the group comes to a consensus about the best name for conflict, make the following statement: "We have just made a group decision. As we go forward, we will see whether this decision has resolved a conflict or merely buried it. For the next two days, our word for conflict will be [the word the group has chosen]."

Go to the flip chart where you have written "The Conflict Management Skills Workshop," cross out the word *conflict,* and write in the word the group has chosen. This is the word you will use instead of *conflict* whenever possible during the two-day workshop.

If the group cannot come to a consensus within the allotted time, declare a deadlock. Note how important language is to people, and thank participants for their hard work. Especially note the contribution of the person or persons holding out. By insisting on what they consider important, they have kept conflict from being swept under the rug.

Note that time will not allow you to figure out a better name, so you will use the relatively neutral term *conflict* for the remainder of the workshop. Everyone else, of course, may use whatever term works best for him or her.

Commentary: Tell participants that they are all experts in conflict. (I will use the word *conflict* for this discussion, but you should use the word that the group has agreed upon.) We all have experience in this area. We all have knowledge and opinions about conflict. And we all have feelings about what works best when dealing with conflict. The idea in this workshop is not to tell you about conflict as much as it is to learn from our fellow experts and come to an agreement about how we can make conflict a positive experience for us at work.

Tell the group that your expertise is in ensuring that the workshop goes well. You will ensure that participants follow the agenda and you will track the time. They are the ones who will make the decisions about what comes out of your two days together.

WAYS OF SEEING

Commentary: Explain that there are many things to get into a conflict over than merely what to name something. Another useful name for conflict is *difference.* Sometimes people get into a conflict when they have a different way of looking at the world.

Tell the group that although some differences—such as religion or culture—may be obvious to us, it is good to remember that there are many other ways of seeing things that people can get into a conflict about. Since we all come from different backgrounds—whether we grew up next door to one another or on opposite sides of the world—we all have different experiences that shape the way we look at things.

❓ Discussion Ask participants to call out some things that shape the way we view the world and to write as many as possible on a flip chart.

If people generally respond by saying culture or language, ask them, "What are some things about culture that shape the way we see the world?" Try to elicit specific answers such as ceremonies, beliefs, schooling, or traditions. There are no wrong answers, but people should be as specific as possible.

 Story and Discussion: *To Bag or Not to Bag, Good Manners,* **and** *The Lilliputian Egg Wars*

Point out that even seemingly minor cultural differences can take us by surprise.

Tell a story that illustrates how a minor cultural difference can cause surprising behavior. A first-person example from your own experience is best, or you can use or adapt Story 1.1: *To Bag or Not to Bag* or Story 1.2: *Good Manners.*

TO BAG OR NOT TO BAG

I grew up in southern California and now live in the Philadelphia area. In southern California, when you go to the grocery store, the checker or someone else from the store will put your groceries in the bag for you. It doesn't matter whether you are in a fancy store or not. In Philadelphia, until recently, the custom has been for customers to put their own groceries in the bag. I have lived in Philly for ten years. On a recent trip to San Diego, I went with a friend to the supermarket.

As the checker began to ring up our food, I moved to the end of the checkout counter, grabbed a bag, and started to put my groceries away. It seemed to me to be a perfectly normal thing to do. The checker stopped checking, and my friend's mouth fell open. Neither spoke, until the checker said, "Is everything okay?"

It's all she could think of to say, since she had to be polite to the customer, and since my behavior was so bizarre.

"Is everything okay?"

I was just as startled. Nothing else came to mind, so I apologized. "Sorry," I said, and quickly took a step away from the groceries.

Everything went back to normal—the "right" way for these people on the other coast—and when the checker was finished ringing up the order, she put the food into bags for us. As she was bagging, I explained that where I come from people bag their own groceries, and my friend and the checker shook their heads and clucked sympathetically.

The truth, I think, is that one way is not morally superior to the other. Some people may like to bag their own groceries, while others may not. It might only be what they get used to. We certainly weren't going to have a conflict about it, but sometimes, customs are exactly what we fight about.

GOOD MANNERS

A Saudi businessperson was furious because the CEO of the company he was coming to visit in the United States did not meet him at the airport. It ruined the trip and strained relations between the two companies. The U.S. CEO thought that the Saudi visitor would want to go to his hotel and relax or freshen up before meeting anyone.

Even after a North American explained that it was common for U.S. businesspeople to make their own way from the airport to their meetings, the guest could not get over his impression that he was dealing with extremely rude people.

Can you think of instances when customs or rules that might not matter in the larger picture have been misunderstood and caused problems for you? Remember, this doesn't have to be between people from different countries or different coasts. It can be equally confusing between people who live together or who work together.

To sum up, tell participants the brief version of Story 1.3: *The Lilliputian Egg Wars*. You can summarize the story, read it aloud, or give it to them to read and comment on.

Facilitate a discussion about the stories.

Explain that people sometimes have conflict over differences that may seem inconsequential to outsiders. Even serious issues with serious outcomes can seem minor or easy to fix if you are not in the middle of them. An example may be the wars in the Balkans.

Many people in the United States have trouble understanding how people who had been neighbors for many years could suddenly turn into mortal enemies. Likewise, many Europeans are confused about the debates over gun control, abortion, and the Confederate flag currently being waged in the United States. Explain that is the reason why people in conflict often ask an outsider to help them sort things out.

WAYS OF KNOWING

Commentary: Put the group at ease by telling participants that you are not going to discuss hot topics such as gun control, abortion, or the Confederate flag. However, remind them that each person's reaction to that list is based on what she or he feels is the truth.

Truth

 Discussion Ask participants, "How do we know that something is true?" Write their responses on a flip chart and post it. If the group is having trouble thinking of responses, prompt participants with a suggestion of your own.

Expect answers such as:

We see it for ourselves. *We experience it.*

We trust the person who tells it to us. *It's in the Bible*

It is important not to get into a discussion about which of these sources of truth is the correct one. Be sure that your response to each remark is as neutral as possible. The point you would like to make is that each one of us feels strongly about our source or sources of truth, and that these sources may vary widely from one reasonable person to another.

THE LILLIPUTIAN EGG WARS

". . . the primitive way of breaking eggs before we eat them, was upon the larger end: but his present Majesty's grandfather, while he was a boy, going to eat an egg, and breaking it according to the ancient practice, happened to cut one of his fingers. Whereupon the Emperor, his father published an edict, commanding all his subjects, upon great penalties, to break the smaller end of their eggs. The people so highly resented this law, that our histories tell us there have been six rebellions raised on that account; wherein one emperor lost his life, and another his crown. These civil commotions were constantly fomented by the monarchs of Blefuscu [a neighboring and rival kingdom]; and when they were quelled, the exiles always fled for refuge to that empire. It is computed, that eleven thousand persons have, at several times, suffered death, rather than submit to break their eggs at the smaller end. Many hundred large volumes have been published upon this controversy: but the books of the Big-Endians have been long forbidden, and the whole party rendered incapable by law of holding employments. During the course of these troubles, the emperors of Blefuscu did frequently expostulate by their ambassadors, accusing us of making a schism in religion, by offending against a fundamental doctrine of our great prophet Lustrog, in the fifty-fourth chapter of the *Brundecral*. . . . This, however, is thought to be a mere strain upon the text: for the words are these; *That all true believers shall break their eggs at the convenient end . . .*"

—From *Gulliver's Travels* by Jonathan Swift, 1726

THE SECOND LOOK

Commentary: Tell the group that one method for checking the facts is to look at the truth a second time or from a different angle. As an example, you may use one or all of the following stories: Story 1.4: *The Farmer on the Porch,* Story 1.5: *The Pink Moment,* or Story 1.6: *The Colored Ball.*

Story and Discussion: *The Farmer on the Porch, The Pink Moment, and The Colored Ball*

Your workshop participants know that when they listen to a story they are supposed to relax and enjoy themselves. So introduce Story 1.4: *The Farmer on the Porch,* Story 1.5: *The Pink Moment,* and Story 1.6: *The Colored Ball* by saying, "I am going to tell you three short stories about different ways of knowing what is true." This lets participants know how to receive the information you are about to send. They will get ready to hear a story. Tell the stories to the group one right after the other. This helps people to see many different ways to take a second look at what they know to be true in an entertaining, non-threatening way.

THE FARMER ON THE PORCH

There is an old story that I heard when I was a kid about a reporter who was driving through the southern United States. I don't know whether you have ever been in the Deep South, but it is beautiful country. This man was driving on an old red-dirt road, winding his way through a grove of trees. Here and there he would pass a little farm or deserted filling station. It was hot and humid and buggy—the kind of day that makes you want to sit as still as you can in the shade with a tall glass of cold lemonade.

Our reporter was looking for something to write about—a bit of local color. He drove past a little house—no paint on the gray boards, sagging roof, and an old man tipped back in his chair on the weather-beaten front porch. The old man was rocking gently in the heat and had attached a long wooden pole to a garden hoe. This invention allowed the old man to rock on the porch and hoe his garden at the same time.

The reporter smiled. "A lazy day in the Old South," he thought. He had his local color. The story goes that as the reporter drove by, something made him look in his side mirror for one last picture. That is when he noticed that the old man had no legs.

A second look turned what would have been a patronizing story about a stereotype into a story of courage, strength, and indomitable will.

≈

What the reporter saw the first time was true. He had seen it for himself. If we knew this reporter to be reliable and he hadn't looked back, we would have believed the truth of his first story. What the reporter saw when he looked back was true. He had seen it for himself. If we choose to believe the reporter, then this becomes true.

Often, what makes what we see hold different truths is the meaning we decide to put on it. When we add the layers of meaning that come from our customs, beliefs, and experience, the story becomes more or less true for us.

If one of us had seen one story and another had seen the other, we might even have something to fight about.

THE PINK MOMENT

Things can be different depending upon where you are standing, and even what you choose to look at. I grew up in southern California. For some reason, many people in the rest of the United States think that Californians are a little strange. Some of us are.

Just north of Los Angeles in the hills overlooking the Pacific Ocean is the town of Ojai. Ojai, California, is a pretty little place that has attracted artists and creative types since the end of the 1800s. It has been a while since I've been there, so I don't know if they still wait for the Pink Moment, but when I was there last, people were still proud of an interesting local tradition.

When the sun sets over the Pacific, people in Ojai wander outside. Stores shut down, or at least all work stops for awhile. Everybody is outside to watch the sun go down. It is beautiful, but a funny thing separates the locals from the visitors. People who are from Ojai come outside for the sunset, but as soon as the sun touches the edge of the ocean, they all turn their backs on it.

Anybody know why?

The Pink Moment, of course. When the sun is going down in Ojai, people who want to see the Pink Moment turn away from the sunset and watch the foothills to the east turn from green or gold to a faint, flickering rose.

THE COLORED BALL

Imagine that there is a huge ball suspended in the middle of the room. This side of the ball is red. This side of the ball is blue. If we had a class discussion about the ball, and I asked someone from this side of the room what color the ball is, she would say, "red." If I asked someone from this side of the room, he would say, "blue." If I spun the ball very fast, someone might say, "When the ball sits still, it is red (or blue, if you are one of *those* people) and when it spins, it is purple."

How could someone on the blue side convince someone on the red side that the blue side is right?

Have them come over to see this side.

And what happens if someone from one side goes over to the other side to get them to come over?

They see what is true for the other side.

Right. And the next challenge for this person who has seen both sides of the ball is to convince everybody else on both sides that things may be different depending upon where you are standing.

Story and Discussion: *The Blind Men and the Elephant*
Explain that sometimes it isn't the truth that we fight about but rather how we organize the truth so that it makes sense to us.
Tell Story 1.7: *The Blind Men and the Elephant.*

 Discussion Ask participants:

"How could the five blind men have worked this out?"

"Why didn't they?"

"Does what happened with the blind men and the elephant ever occur in business?"

"What can we do about it?"

"What happens if the guy who thinks that an elephant is like a leaf is the boss? How do we handle that?"

There are no correct answers to these questions. Encourage as many responses as possible. Do not comment except to encourage. There is no need to reach consensus on the answers or for you to sum anything up. In fact, you can tell participants that usually the trainer would sum up the conversation for them, but that in this workshop you want them to reach their own decisions. If you like, you can ask for a volunteer to do the summing up for you.

WAYS OF LEARNING

Explain that although belief systems cause us to see the world differently from one another, sometimes the way we process information can differ as well.

 Story and Discussion: *Losing Sara*
Ask the participants to read Story 1.8: *Losing Sara* in their copies of the Participant Workbook, and then talk about the questions in small groups.

THE BLIND MEN AND THE ELEPHANT

One more story about how we can be convinced of competing truths . . . Anybody ever hear of the story of the blind men and the elephant? The story is about five blind friends who decide to learn about the elephant—a creature that they had heard of but that they had never experienced firsthand. The five split up to find out what they could about the elephant and then came back to meet and compare notes.

"The elephant," said the first blind man, "is very much like a snake."

"No," said the second. "The elephant is very much like a rope."

The other friends had different replies. One said an elephant is like a large leaf, another said it was like the trunk of a tree, and the last one said that the elephant is like an immense wall.

≈♠

Of course, we know that one was feeling the trunk, another the tail, another the ear, and so on. In the story, the blind men get into a terrible fight.

How could they have avoided this?

By talking with one another. By listening. Etc.

Each blind man in the story had become a specialist on one part of the elephant and refused to acknowledge that there may be something that he did not know.

His perspective was determined by where he began and ended his experience.

All of the blind men were right. Together, if they figured out how to learn from one another, they would have also been right—and they would have benefited from their differing viewpoints to know more about elephants than any single one of them could by acting alone.

Does this ever happen in business?

What can we do about it?

What happens if the guy who thinks an elephant is like a leaf is the boss?

LOSING SARA

Four good friends—Sara, Art, Mihi, and Margaret—went into business together. Art was good at encouraging people to work well together and had the most business experience, so it was decided that he would head things up. Sara liked doing research, so tracking the competition and designing new products became her job. Margaret was highly energetic and well-liked by clients. She became the salesperson. Mihi had marketing experience and was very detail-oriented. She took over creating sales materials and keeping everyone and everything on track.

Their meetings were interesting, to say the least. Margaret and Art liked to talk a lot. The two of them would often monopolize the meetings, excitedly interrupting one another with their ideas. They were funny and enjoyed one another's company. Mihi would join in the joking but otherwise kept quiet during the meetings. She would take notes and occasionally interject to sum things up or move things along. It was the most difficult for Sara. Her office was in another city, and she would join the meetings by telephone. Nobody could see her and she had trouble knowing what was going on during the meetings.

Sara would usually call into the meetings with some carefully thought-out plan. When she presented her idea, Art would open things up for discussion. He and Margaret would then springboard one idea off another one until the plan didn't look a thing like what Sara had presented. Because she was naturally quieter than Margaret and Art, and because she had to telephone in to the meetings, Sara often felt as if her ideas weren't being heard.

When Art and Margaret would take Sara's ideas to the most extreme level, Mihi would remind them that time was almost up and that there were other things that needed to be talked about that day.

One day, Sara dropped a bombshell at the weekly meeting. She waited until the roundtable at the end of the session. This was a time when Art would go around to each person and ask how she thought the meeting had gone. Usually, people would say something like, "Great! I think we have generated a lot of good ideas today."

At this particular roundtable, Margaret had gone first. She thanked everybody for their help with a sales proposal that she had in front of a new client and said how much fun it was to work with people who cared so much about one another.

Art added that the best thing about their work together was that they all got along so well and loved to collaborate on creative solutions. Then, he asked Sara to take her turn at the roundtable.

Sara hesitated and took a deep breath. Her voice over the telephone sounded tight. "You know how important this business and all of you are to me," she said, "but I need you to know that as of the end of the month, I'll be leaving our company." Sara went on to say that she had already contacted the company's attorney to clarify the process of rescinding her partnership shares, and that she wanted her departure to be amicable.

The rest of the team was stunned. Finally, Art spoke. "Sara, please don't rush into anything. I'm sure that we can work out whatever is bothering you. Why don't you fly up here so that we can talk face-to-face?"

Margaret's eyes teared up. "I know it's been hard being so far away, Sara. I'm sure we can work things out if we all get together."

Sara answered quietly.

"I have been thinking about this for some time and even talked it over a little with Mihi. Most of the company's stuff is already packed up to ship back to you. I need to work with people I can see. I know this is for the best."

Margaret and Art tried to get Sara to give them a reason for quitting. Mihi busied herself with her notepad. Finally, the call came to an uncomfortable end with Sara promising to think about it and agreeing to talk with Art by telephone later in the week.

When they got off the telephone, Art turned to Mihi.

"Mihi?"

"All she ever told me was that she needed her ideas to be more respected. I said she needed to speak up around you two or else just do her own thing and hope you guys went along."

Margaret didn't want to talk. She said she was too upset.

Art told his two partners that he was going for a walk, got his coat, and left.

ઽ.

There is a lot going on with these people. One thing that may be getting in the way of the four friends is the different way that each of them processes information. People learn in a variety of ways that may change depending upon the specific situation in which they find themselves.

Art, for example, waits for someone else's good idea then manipulates it. He bounces ideas off Margaret or anyone else who will join in until he is comfortable with what he has learned. Then he goes "outside the box," thinking of extreme variations on what he understands from the original proposal. He has fun doing this and doesn't particularly care what comes of it. One thing that Art knows for certain is that his way works for him. When the brainstorming session is over, there will always be more good ideas than he knows what to do with.

Margaret follows Art's lead and enjoys seeing him work. She sometimes wishes he would slow down. She thinks that some good ideas may be left in the dust if they move too quickly. Days after the meeting, Art is still coming up with new approaches. Margaret teases him about it, since she and the others have usually moved on to something else.

"Earth to Art" is a common joke among the four partners.

Margaret learns by testing and revising Art's ideas until they become practical. She does this quickly and then tells Mihi about it. Mihi figures out the potential costs and other details and tries to explain Margaret's results to the others.

Art and Margaret care deeply about their friends and feel terrible about what they see as their failure with Sara. They know they need Sara's careful planning and analysis to get things done. Sara enjoys her partners' energy but worries about how unmethodical they are. She would like, for a change, to be able to present an idea fully before Art takes off on his flights of fancy. Sara's quiet nature makes long-distance communication with her more outgoing colleagues that much more difficult.

Nobody seems to notice that Sara carefully studies several approaches and probable outcomes before presenting her ideas. Often, Art and Margaret come up with ideas that Sara has already analyzed and discarded. Recently, Sara has begun to think that only Mihi understands the hard work that goes into her proposals.

Mihi loves her job. It is fun being with her friends, and she knows she can make sense out of whatever they come up with. She worries a little about the company's lack of direction and wants them all to see the same big picture that she does, but Mihi knows they will come around if she plans carefully enough. Although she doesn't know what to do about Sara, Mihi is convinced that she can figure out a way for the company to work, no matter what. When Sara first spoke to her about her problem communicating long distance, Mihi went online and ordered several books about conflict and communication. She plans to speak privately with each partner over the next few weeks so that they can develop a master plan.

ન**

Small Group Discussion: We all have ways of learning that have worked best for us. Your approach to learning and to communicating information has been developed over a period of years. Usually, we each end up with an approach that works for us, one that we have been rewarded for in some way.

Our individual approaches to learning are not set in stone—far from it. Having an idea of how we learn and teach and whether it works for the people we need to communicate with is a good first step to adjusting our style so that it works in a specific situation or with a specific person.

Ask one another: "What should Art, Margaret, Mihi, and Sara do now?"

Talk to the people in your group about whom they are most like—Art, Margaret, Mihi, or Sara? (You can probably answer "a little of each," but for the sake of the exercise, pick the person whose preferences are closest to yours. There is no right answer or one best preference.)

Whom are you most like?

Whom are you least like?

Trainer Tip: A powerful alternative to Story 1.8: *Losing Sara* is the *Learning Style Inventory.* In approximately one hour, people can learn about and compare their own learning styles and discuss how not knowing about these differences can lead to conflict. For ordering information, see the Toolbox section.

WAYS OF LIVING

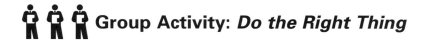 **Group Activity: *Do the Right Thing***

Type
Role Play

Purpose
People have fun with this exercise, even if it frustrates them. The active, emotional involvement of the group makes a strong and memorable impression. The exercise gives individuals a shared experience of dealing with invisible differences, which they can use as a reference point when working together in the future.

Equipment Needed
- Flip-chart paper
- Markers
- Handout 1.2: Group One Instructions
- Handout 1.3: Group Two Instructions
- Handout 1.4: Group Three Instructions
- Handout 1.5: Group Four Instructions

Preparation
Make copies of Handout 1.2: Group One Instructions, Handout 1.3: Group Two Instructions, Handout 1.4: Group Three Instructions, and Handout 1.5: Group Four Instructions. Write problem statement on flip-chart paper.

The problem statement should be something that people have an opinion about, but that most people would be comfortable talking about at work. You may use one of the following problem statements or come up with one of your own:

"How late is too late when you are late for a business meeting?"

"What is the best/worst program on television?"

"Which movie should we go to see?"

"What should we have for lunch?"

"What is the best thing to do on a Saturday morning?"

Time
20 minutes

Introduction
Tell the workshop participants that you have a problem for them to solve together. Read the problem statement from the flip chart.

Activity
Instructions
Divide the participants into four groups of equal size. Give each group the handout for their group. Tell participants not to share the information with the other groups until after the exercise.

 Trainer Tip: If your workshop group is very small, you can do this with as few as two groups. In this case, use the instructions for group one and group two. Either change the instructions to eliminate the reference to the other groups, or explain to the people in the workshop that more groups are used for larger numbers of participants.

Instruct the groups to go to separate rooms or areas where they cannot hear each other as they discuss their instructions. Take care when answering questions from each group so that the other groups cannot hear you.

Bring the separate groups together and announce that everyone will now work together on the problem statement for at least five minutes.

Allow participants to work together on the problem statement for five minutes. You may need to prompt people to join in the discussion.

Debriefing
At the end of five minutes, ask the participants to drop their roles. Facilitate a discussion about what just took place.

Use the following seven steps to encourage discussion:

1. Start by asking each group to tell what happened during the exercise.
2. Ask the participants how it felt to conform to different rules of behavior.
3. Ask each group how it felt to deal with the other groups.
4. Let the explanations for different behavior emerge.
5. Let the observers speak.

6. Ask questions about what they could have done to communicate better.

7. Ask whether it would have helped to know the different ground rules ahead of time.

Often, people will make statements about individuals, such as "Pat was cowardly. He wouldn't make eye contact or respond when I spoke to him," or "Elena was uncooperative and made it hard to solve the problem. She kept saying that we had to stop the exercise." Make the point that now that we know the motivation for these actions, they do not seem to be as "wrong." In fact, what happened is that the group saw a specific behavior (such as no eye contact) and gave it meaning based on what they are used to.

This exercise has given everyone a chance to belong to a culture that does not understand another culture. We made up rules for behavior that people were forced to follow without explanation. Because we learned them as rules, they quickly became important to us. Since these new rules broke the rules that other people accept, they bothered people who did not know that the behavior had a different meaning in another culture.

It is important for us to try to look behind a person's presentation—things such as tone of voice, posture, eye contact, pace, loudness, or definition of personal space—to see what the real intent or need of the other person is. He may be struggling to get through to you just as much as you are struggling to get through to him, but you both may be blocked because you are interpreting one another's actions based on different sets of rules.

Instead of allowing customs to upset you further, learn about the differences in the other person's culture in matters of communication and conflict. If you guess that she is from the same culture as you but still cannot understand her choice of actions, ask her gentle questions about what it is that she needs to get out of your work together.

Finally, sum up the discussion and ask participants whether they agree with your summary.

GROUP ONE INSTRUCTIONS

Use everything that you know about conflict to work with group two and group three on the situation written on the flip chart.

Group four will not speak during this exercise. They are here only to observe and take notes.

GROUP TWO INSTRUCTIONS

Use everything that you know about conflict to work with group one and group three on the situation written on the flip chart. Group four will not speak during this exercise. They are here only to observe and take notes.

As a member of group two, you belong to a unique cultural group that has a special set of behaviors. During the exercise, you need to follow these behaviors very strictly.

Group Two's Behaviors:

❏ Women can speak to any man or woman.

❏ Men can speak to any man.

❏ Men can only speak to a woman in their own group if spoken to first by that woman.

❏ Men can only respond to women in the other groups through a woman in their own group.

❏ Direct eye contact is considered extremely rude.

❏ Smiling when saying maybe means no.

GROUP THREE INSTRUCTIONS

Use everything that you know about conflict to work with group one and group two on the situation written on the flip chart. Group four will not speak during this exercise. They are here only to observe and take notes.

As a member of group three, you belong to a unique cultural group that has a special set of beliefs. During the exercise, you need to follow these beliefs very strictly.

Group Three's Beliefs:

❏ You believe strongly that any time anyone is in a training exercise that goes more than three minutes beyond its allotted time, it will shorten that person's life span by five years.

❏ You, as a member of group three, care about the welfare of your fellow human beings above everything else.

GROUP FOUR INSTRUCTIONS

Use everything that you know about conflict as you observe groups one, two, and three working together on the situation described on the flip chart. You must not speak or offer any help during this exercise. You are here only to observe and take notes. It may be best if you and your group members split up and watch specific people or groups during the exercise.

You may want to use this checklist to help you take notes.

Things to watch for:

❏ Displays of frustration or impatience
❏ Displays of open hostility or anger
❏ Name calling
❏ Uses of humor (positive or negative)
❏ Asking questions about why people are behaving differently from usual
❏ Attempts to explain why people are behaving differently from usual
❏ What incidents cause what reactions
❏ Any juicy quotes that may illustrate how the exercise is going
❏ Anything else of interest

Trainer Tip: Here are three quick examples from my own training experience that may help clarify the way that we assign meaning to different actions.

First Example: The Long Good-bye

After a long day of training new businesspeople in Shanghai, China, I was getting into my car to go back to the hotel. My host for the day came hurrying out of the training center and grabbed my hand. He shook my hand rapidly up and down and said, "Xie xie! Thank you so much for coming and spending so much time with us!"

I had one foot in the car and the other on the curb. American style, I pumped his hand once and said, "The pleasure was all mine. I have learned so much from your students. Thank you!"

I tried to go, but he tightened his grip and kept pumping. "No! Thank you!"

"Thank you!" I said, "This has been wonderful."

He wouldn't let go. "Thank you," he said again.

We traded many more thank-you's until I realized that as the honored guest, it was necessary for me to allow the last thank-you to go to my host.

"Thank you," he said again, taking his turn.

"Think nothing of it," I said. "Good-bye."

He dropped my hand and I got into the car. We drove off and my grateful host waved until we turned the corner.

There were two sets of rules in conflict here. From my European/ North American perspective, I had been trapped in a slightly comical, but also mildly awkward social situation. I was in danger of being locked in a competition with my host and had no rules to help me out of it. My host, on the other hand, was equally stuck. Although he was too polite to say anything, he may very well have been thinking, "What's wrong with this guy? Didn't his mother teach him any manners at all? What a hick!"

Of course, my host wasn't trying to "win" anything. He was just behaving well. On the other hand, I wasn't being rude—I just didn't know how to get out of the handshake and into the car. Neither set of rules is morally superior, more effective, or better in any way. Sometimes, however, we become so accustomed to our own set of made-up rules that we think they are more normal than somebody else's set of made-up rules.

Second Example: Here's Looking at You

While a workshop group was talking about the Do the Right Thing exercise not too long ago, a factory worker raised his hand and told a story that sums the exercise up very well.

"I am from Trinidad and Tobago," he said. "In my country, it is rare to look someone straight in the eyes, particularly for men and women. In the United States, it seems like it is very common. Back home, when I look straight at a woman and she looks straight back at me, it means she is very attracted to me. Here, in this country, it means she is being honest with me. I didn't know this difference when I first came to America. Here, every woman I met looked at me straight in the eyes. After one week in the United States, I wrote a letter home to my friend and said, 'I must be the luckiest, most handsome man in America. Every woman I look at wants me. Too bad I am so shy.'"

In the Do the Right Thing exercise, some of the players embrace rules that make them behave in ways that most of us do not understand. In fact, the way they behave may have an unpleasant meaning according to the rules that we do understand.

Sometimes, conflict arises or is intensified even though people are unaware that they are adding confusion or that what they are doing is insulting. This conflict is not limited to large culture gaps. It can also occur when one person's definition of acceptable behavior is in opposition to another person's definition.

Third Example: The Shout Heard 'Round the World

United States businesspeople who work with British businesspeople often comment on how much quieter their partners from across the pond are when speaking in a meeting or in front of a group.

I spent several days in Philadelphia engaged in meetings with three English South African clients. They had gone out to dinner in the city the night before and were convinced that they must have done something to anger the woman who had served them their meal.

"She yelled at us," they said.

"What did she say?" I asked.

"What can I get you?"

I explained that many North Americans, especially those from the East Coast, tend to speak more loudly and more rapidly than do people from almost anywhere else. I told them that when I moved east from California, I had to figure the same thing out. What the woman at the restaurant wanted to let them know was that she was excited to see them. What the South Africans heard was an angry voice. Once they learned the local custom, they were no longer worried or offended.

 TRAINER Tip: Two thought-provoking methods for discussing this exercise are to use the "left-hand column" exercise and the "ladder of inference," which were developed by Chris Argyris and his colleagues. Both of these approaches help people look at what is being said or done and the assumptions and beliefs that lie behind them. Clear, simple explanations and exercises using both of these concepts can be found in *The Fifth Discipline Fieldbook,* which is listed in the Toolbox section.

WAYS OF SEEING CONFLICT

Commentary: Tell the group that the last method of seeing that you will explore with them is called "ways of seeing conflict."

What we believe about conflict itself—whether we see it as good or bad, contest or collaboration—often determines how we will act in a conflict situation. Show participants Flip Chart 1.2: Two Ways of Seeing Conflict, and provide a quick overview of each of the following ways of seeing.

Win, Lose, or Draw

Commentary: We often view conflict as a contest that must have a clear winner and loser. The only other alternative to winning or losing is some type of draw. The only strategy available to us when we see conflict this way is to do everything we can to ensure that the other side loses. This type of contest often takes place when we negotiate. When negotiating, people often carefully choose how much to reveal to the other party. They tell the people on the other side only enough to keep them interested and withhold information that might help their opponent to win.

 Discussion Ask participants:

"Is it ever okay to hide information from someone when you are working to win a conflict?" "Is it ever okay to lie?"

If group members believe that it is sometimes okay to hide information or to lie, ask them to give examples of situations—either made up or from their own experience—when it may be the right thing to do.

Two Ways of Seeing Conflict

1. *A Contest:*
   - *Win*
   - *Lose*
   - *Draw*

2. *A Problem to Solve Together:*
   - *Make It Even*
   - *Make It Bigger*
   - *Make It Different*

Facilitator: Remember that your role here is not to convince the group of what you believe to be right. You are also not here to talk about or enforce company policy. If you feel the need to remind them of company policy from time to time, do so as gently as possible: "Of course, company policy says that we must [fill in the blank], but for the purposes of the workshop, we are exploring every alternative that seems reasonable to each of us."

Trainer Tip: If participants cannot come up with an example that illustrates when it might be permissible to lie, give them an example of some ambiguous situations, such as:

- *When telling the truth may cause someone to be harmed.* For example, your chief executive officer (CEO) has just received a call from one of your company's largest and most difficult customers. He is furious because he has been billed three times for the same service. This is not the first time this has happened, and he has threatened to take his business to another company. The CEO has told you to "find out whoever is causing the problem and get rid of him or her." You know it is one of your new clerks, but you feel she has improved since the billing problems occurred. You tell the CEO the whole thing was a computer problem that has been fixed and that it should not happen again.

- *Lying to keep from having to do something you feel is wrong.* For example, your sales manager has told you to sell the last 300 pieces of a product that you know is below your guaranteed quality standard. The manager is convinced that if you hide the defects, the pieces should be easy to get rid of. You have objected to selling the inferior product, but your sales manager is insistent. Instead of trying to sell it, you tell the manager that you have called around already, but people seem to have plenty of product on hand.

- *Lying to keep someone from losing face.* For example, your team has worked hard to put out the company's annual report. It is generally agreed on that it is the best-looking report yet. The problem is that you need to call the board members and tell them that the report is late and that their meeting must be rescheduled. You know that the report is late because the CEO forgot to take it with him to proofread when he went on his last business trip. You tell one particularly angry board member that the report is late because of a machine problem at your printer.

- *Lying to keep from losing money.* For example, you scratched your rental car when trying to get the keys out of it with a coat hanger. When the rental car agent notices the scratches, you say that the car was scratched when you got it.

- *Deciding to always tell the truth, but to not offer information unless specifically asked for it.* For example, you have always told the sales group you manage that if you know of something going on in the company, they will know as well. You have just come from a meeting where you found out that the sales force will be laid off in December. One of your salespeople asks what was discussed at the meeting. You say, "We went over payroll numbers."

Commentary: Wrap up the discussion by saying that we all have a different bottom line when it comes to what we will or will not share when we are in a win, lose, or draw situation.

It is easier to make choices about what we tell people with whom we have differences if we can look at conflict in a more constructive way.

Make It Even, Make It Bigger, or Make It Different

 Discussion Ask participants:

"Have any of you heard of 'win/win'?"

"What does that mean to you?"

"How do you do it?"

Ask participants for examples of win/win solutions. They may be solutions that have worked, are working, or (in the opinion of a participant) might work if someone would give these solutions a try. The examples may come from work or elsewhere.

 Facilitator: Write the examples on a piece of flip-chart paper. You will need to come up with at least seven or eight examples to use later when discussing responses to conflict.

TRAINER Tip: If participants are quiet during large group discussions, separate them into smaller groups of five to ten people, and tell them that they have five minutes to report back with at least one favorite example from each group. During the small group discussions, be sure to walk around and listen to what is going on. You may get ideas for examples that the groups do not report back on.

Commentary: After the discussion, explain that there are several methods for approaching conflict that ensure that everyone comes out a little bit ahead. The three methods that we are going to discuss are called "make it even," "make it bigger," or "make it different."

As you explain the approaches, be sure to integrate examples that the group came up with from the win/win discussion. For example: "Mario's example fits very nicely into the make-it-different category." Even better, after explaining all three, ask something like, "Where does Liam's example fit: 'make it even,' 'make it bigger,' or 'make it different'?"

Make It Even

Commentary: This is the type of compromise many of us learn to use when we are children. It is splitting something up even-steven, or at least in a way that we hope makes everybody happy. (Or at least in a way that we hope makes everybody less *un*happy.)

Story and Discussion: ***The Shared Resource*** and ***My Dad and the Last Brownie***

Use an example of an even-steven solution that was used at work, or use or adapt Story 1.9: *The Shared Resource* or Story 1.10: *My Dad and the Last Brownie.*

THE SHARED RESOURCE

When we think of conflict as a win/lose situation, we have only one of three possible outcomes: win, lose, or draw. When we think of it as a win/win situation, we have to use different strategies: make it even, make it bigger, or make it different.

Here is what I mean by make it even. We can both win if we are fighting about something that can be split down the middle, or otherwise divided in a way that makes everyone happy.

Let us say there is a worker whose salary is split between two departments. The head of one department uses two-thirds of the worker's time, and the other is angry because she only gets one-third of the worker's time but pays for half. How can they make this even?

Regulate the worker's hours to ensure that the time is split 50/50.

Change the percentage paid by each to accurately reflect the allocation of the worker's time.

Charge each department according to the hours actually worked in each department.

Etc.

MY DAD AND THE LAST BROWNIE

I grew up in the middle of a family of six kids. I don't think we gave our parents too much grief, but with eight people in the house, there were naturally things to disagree about.

We all know the classic complaint of children to a parent, "He's looking at me!" When I was about five years old, my older brother actually complained to our mother that I was not only looking at him, but that I was looking at his food. Hard not to with six kids—the oldest was age nine, the youngest age one—crammed around the kitchen table.

Needless to say, Mom became adept at knowing who got which color drinking glass, whose turn it "really" was to do dishes, and any number of other crucial decisions. She had the answer to all of these judicial questions, but for some reason, it was my father who ruled on cases where there was no clear precedent.

Somewhere along the line, Dad picked up an interesting even-steven solution for the problem of two kids and one last brownie. "Here," he said, giving the knife to my brother, "You cut the brownie in half." Then he looked at me, "You get to pick who gets which half."

You never saw such careful cutting in your life. Both kids became involved in solving the problem of being certain that the solution was even-steven.

And Dad was off the hook.

Discussion

Ask the group for additional examples and to categorize some of their examples from the win/win discussion as make-it-even solutions.

Make It Bigger

Commentary: Explain that sometimes cutting something up even-steven is only going to put a lid on conflict for a short time.

If each person believes that the whole brownie is rightfully his or hers, then splitting it may appease some for a while, but nobody is going to be thrilled with the outcome.

 Discussion Ask participants: "What do you think will happen the next time that there is a brownie shortage?"

Explain that sometimes there is only one brownie, and making it bigger is the best solution. When we say we are going to make it bigger, we do not mean that we can grow the brownie. What we mean is that we are going to get more brownies. The idea is that if there is not a sufficient amount of something to go around, we need to get more of it.

This could be how the smorgasbord was invented. When two people cannot agree on one of two choices, they include both choices in their final decision. At the smorgasbord, both people agree that they need to eat but cannot agree on the entrée.

Here is a business example: The vice presidents of sales and operations are arguing in an executive committee meeting. It seems that sales is promising things that operations cannot deliver. Or, if you believe the sales vice president, operations is making sales look bad by not coming through on customer commitments.

What they agree on is that there is a problem and that they need to keep the customers happy. How can they make this bigger?

Include one another in planning.

Right. A little more complicated than merely cutting something in two. What our two vice presidents need to do is make each of their processes bigger to include the other process.

 Discussion Ask participants: "What are some examples from business when a conflict over resources can be reasonably dealt with by getting more resources?"

 Story and Discussion: *Rueben and Laurel*
This is not always an easy one to come up with. If the group seems stuck, ask them to read Story 1.11: *Rueben and Laurel,* and then ask them for their ideas.

RUEBEN AND LAUREL

Two managers, Rueben and Laurel, have worked together for five years and have become good friends. Rueben is a top salesperson and Laurel heads up the company's customer service unit. They often drop into one another's offices to talk over problems. Both of them look forward to working on projects together and tend to agree about what to do in various business situations. Although they don't generally socialize outside of the office, they have met one another's spouses at company functions and always talk about getting everybody together for dinner some weekend. They consider themselves friends and allies.

In a corporate consolidation, the two managers' departments have been merged, and Laurel has been put in charge. Rueben now reports to her. Laurel has been told to move out of her office and into what used to be Rueben's area.

There is only one office, and Laurel needs it. Rueben will have to move into a cubicle.

Rueben's main function is sales. He cannot see how he can possibly do a good job from a cubicle. He has carefully set up his office to impress the clients who come in to meet him. It is decorated with sales and golfing awards, and the shelves are full of customer mementos and thank-you gifts.

Laurel has always worked in customer service. She works with most of her customers on the telephone. Her old office was decorated simply: a whiteboard, a few telephone books, and several filing cabinets for customer records. Laurel needs to work in a quiet environment. She also needs a private place where she can meet with her employees, and a secure place for confidential files. Besides, she is now the director of the newly formed department, and she feels it would send the wrong message if she were working in a cubicle while one of her male subordinates had a nice office.

❧

Discussion:
What can Laurel and Rueben do to "make it bigger"?

Hint: Look at what they both need, redefine the problem, and go from there. Remember that how well your solution works will depend largely upon how Laurel and Rueben feel about it.

One make-it-bigger solution for Rueben and Laurel may be to convert the space by building another office.

The people in your workshop may come up with different make-it-bigger solutions. We do not have sufficient information about Rueben and Laurel's budget to know what is reasonable, but that is acceptable for the sake of discussion.

Some of the suggestions the group comes up with for Rueben and Laurel may not be make-it-bigger ideas. They may be make-it-even strategies, such as some type of sharing arrangement. That is fine.

You will also get some make-it-different ideas, such as addressing Laurel's need for respect in her new position and finding out whether there are other ways that Rueben can suitably impress his clients. One solution is for the single office to be made into a conference room that the two share.

Write a summary title on a flip chart for each suggestion the group makes, such as "Share the Office," "Alternative Sales Site," or "Respect for Laurel." When the group has stopped coming up with suggestions, review each title on your flip chart and ask the group whether it is a make-it-even or make-it-bigger solution.

If there are any make-it-different suggestions, tell the group that you will get to those next.

Make It Different

Commentary: Our third way of getting a win for both sides is by making it different. If we think we can only win, lose, or draw in a conflict, then we will not be able to make it different. We need to start thinking outside the box. This is rather like turning our backs on the sunset. Just remember: Intentionally shifting your point of view can pay off in unexpected ways. If you are not hungry, going to the smorgasbord will not help. But sometimes people who are not hungry might end up fighting about what to eat anyway.

If the group has come up with any make-it-different suggestions for Rueben and Laurel, use them to introduce this section. For example:

Sunita's idea for Rueben and Laurel to talk about the personal reasons why each of them needs an office is what we call a make-it-different strategy. We do not mean that we want to make the conflict different when we say, "Make it different." The difference lies in where we choose to place our focus. For example, instead of talking about whether Rueben or Laurel gets the office, we step back far enough to see what lies behind the claims to the office.

Explain that making it different involves beliefs, emotions, the need to save face, and other personal—sometimes hidden—things that make each one of us the person whom we are. When we make it different, we redefine what people are fighting about. Rueben and Laurel's fight may really be about Laurel's needing respect as a woman in her new position. It may be about Rueben's feeling embarrassed that after years of hard work, his new job might look like a step-down.

One way to make it different for Laurel and Rueben is to talk about these hidden parts of their disagreement as friends and colleagues. As they focus on what the other person needs beyond the opening statement of "I need an office," these two people will have a chance at adopting a more creative solution. Rueben and Laurel will also learn about themselves and each other. They will also get better at working out this type of conflict in the future.

Using the group's examples from the Rueben and Laurel discussion, explain that sometimes we need to take a second look or a look from a different vantage point to see what is underlying a person's stance in a conflict.

Review the make-it-different suggestions for Rueben and Laurel. Ask the group for additional examples and ask them to categorize some of the summary titles from the win/win discussion as make-it-different solutions.

 Story and Discussion: *Two Sisters, One Orange*
Ask participants to read Story 1.12: *Two Sisters, One Orange,* to themselves and to answer the questions in small groups of five or six.

TWO SISTERS, ONE ORANGE

In the early 1900s, Mary Parker Follett studied and wrote about conflict and how people could work things out to benefit everyone involved. Follett told this story to explain one approach to conflict.

There were two sisters who both wanted the only orange in the house. As they argued about it, their mother came in and suggested that they cut it in half. They both refused this compromise, so the mother asked them what they needed the orange for. One sister needed the orange to make juice, and half an orange was hardly enough. The other needed the orange for a cake she was baking and needed the entire peel.

Of course, the clever mother helped the two daughters see that they could both be satisfied. One got the peel, the other got the fruit.

Now some hard work for you. Talk to the others in your group and come up with some other situations—from life, from work, from the news, whatever— where things worked out or could work out the same way as Mary Parker Follett's story of the two sisters and the one orange. If you know of a folktale or a story from your childhood that teaches a similar lesson, share that as well.

🏃 Individual Exercise: *What Do I Think About Conflict Right Now?*

There is no need for the groups to report back from their discussions about *Two Sisters and One Orange* at this time. Instead, give them the opportunity to reflect. Ask the participants to read Handout 1.6: Ways of Seeing Conflict.

Once they have finished reading, ask participants to privately fill in Handout 1.7: Reflection Worksheet: What Do I Think About Conflict Right Now? Be sure participants know that their responses will be kept private unless they decide otherwise.

Four reflection sheets (Handouts 1.7, 2.2, 2.4, and 3.22) have been placed at key points in the workshop to give participants a chance to take a moment to slow down their thinking and put what they are experiencing into whatever personal context works best for them.

Introduce the first reflection sheet by saying "Handout 1.7 is a worksheet called What Do I Think About Conflict Right Now? It is the first of a series of four reflection sheets that you can use to think about what you are getting out of this workshop.

"These reflection sheets will help you to organize everything you have been hearing, reading, and talking about up to this point. There is no need to tell anyone what is on your reflection sheet unless you want to. They are for your eyes only—and to give you a chance to take a breath, slow down your brain, and examine old points of view or build new ones. If you have any questions about some of the terms used on the reflection sheet, flip back to Handout 1.6: Ways of Seeing Conflict."

TRAINER TIP: If people working on this reflection sheet get stuck because they cannot remember the details of ways of seeing, ways of learning, ways of knowing, ways of hearing, or ways of seeing conflict, you can do a quick review:

- Ways of Seeing—Do people disagree because of different ways of looking at business or the world around them?

- Ways of Knowing—Do people get into conflicts because both of them know that they are right but they get their proof from different places?

- Ways of Learning—Do differences come up because some people learn by trial and error, some by thinking about things before they act, some by observation, and others through their relationship with other learners?

- Ways of Living—Do disagreements come up between people of different cultures?

- Ways of Seeing Conflict—Do some people disagree because of points of view about whether conflict is a good thing or not? Do differences last a long time because some think conflict is always win/lose/draw and others believe in win/win?

WAYS OF SEEING CONFLICT

We all have our own attitudes and beliefs about the world around us. Sometimes these points of view come from our experiences. Sometimes we have stayed up nights thinking about them. Sometimes we have learned them from someone we respect. Sometimes our points of view just feel "right."

Some points of view are so much a part of us that we cannot begin to think about where they came from. They are just part of whom we are. Often, we believe that these points of view are worth fighting over. They may be, but sometimes a conflict will go on indefinitely because we start fighting about different points of view instead of what the conflict was about in the first place. Once this happens, we can become stuck in a conflict.

To get unstuck, we need to take a look at the point of view that we are defending and figure out where it came from and whether it still makes sense.

Let us say that I cannot go to sleep because I am convinced that there is a monster under the bed. I can check my point of view if I get up and look under the bed. Before I get into a conflict defending a point of view that I am absolutely certain of, it makes sense for me to look under the bed for myself. This way, I can check my point of view to see whether it is based on good information.

I should also check to see whether the information I have leads directly to the point of view. If I hear a noise in the dark, does it always mean that there is a monster under my bed? The information that there is a noise is good information, but I won't know if my point of view makes sense until I get up and turn on the light.

Sometimes our points of view have been with us for so long that it seems like they just grew up out of nowhere—which can make it difficult to figure out where they came from. The following pages cover material that might help you recognize:

- The way you see the world
- The way you are certain that something is true
- The way you learn about new things
- The way you look at conflict itself

Ways of Seeing

Sometimes, people can get into a conflict because they have different ways of looking at the world. Although some differences among people—such as religion or culture—may be obvious to us, it is good to remember that there are plenty of other ways of seeing things that put people in conflict with each other. We all come from different backgrounds, whether we grew up next door to one another or on opposite sides of the world. We all have different experiences that shape the way we look at things. This means that we all end up with different lists of what is important to us. Sometimes we get into conflict over which list is the correct one.

Ways of Knowing

Sometimes we argue or even go to war about what we know to be true. Can there be more than one so-called truth? People have different ways of deciding what is true. There is religious truth; scientific truth; truth that we reason for ourselves; and truth that we learn from a teacher, parent, or some other respected source. Sometimes, we use a combination of these ways of knowing to figure out what is true.

Here are some questions you can ask yourself when you are disagreeing with someone about what is true:

- Where did I get the information that led me to believe that this is true?
- Could someone with different information come to a different conclusion?
- Could someone with the same information come to a different conclusion?
- If the other person's information and sources of information were mine, would I come to the other person's conclusion?

Ways of Learning

People learn differently from one another. Sometimes this can cause confusion, which leads to conflict.

People learn new things either by trial and error, by watching something happen, by thinking about the information offered to them, or by feeling strongly about what is being learned. People also either accept information based on the authority of whoever is telling it to them or like to argue about or think about it on their own and form their opinions that way.

If one person likes to read information and then sit quietly and think about it before coming to a conclusion, while the other person prefers being part of a discussion about the information and coming to a quick conclusion, they might find something to argue about. They might not argue about the conclusion, but they may have trouble agreeing about the best way to get there.

Along the same line, if one person believes strongly that what we learn from a favorite teacher or book is always true, and the other person believes that the best way to figure out what is true is by having a debate, then they may have a difficult time agreeing.

Ways of Seeing Conflict

It is also important to take a good look at how we feel about conflict. Sometimes people see conflict differently from one another and end up fighting about that. Ask yourself the following questions:

- Do I think that conflict is something bad that I should avoid, or something positive that will help me to learn new things?
- Is conflict always a contest, with a clear winner and loser?
- Is conflict ever an opportunity to create something new?

Sometimes people need to agree about how to look at the disagreement before they can look at the disagreement itself. In this workshop, we explore two ways of seeing conflict: "Win, Lose, or Draw" and "Make It Even, Make It Bigger, or Make It Different."

When you learn the way that you look at conflict, you can figure out how to approach it.

Win, lose, or draw is what we call the point of view that in every conflict there are only three possible outcomes for each party. You win, you lose, or there is some kind of a tie. If you see conflict as a win, lose, or draw situation, your best approach is to plan on how you are going to beat the other person. If you do not figure out how to win, you will end up with the short end of the stick.

If you see conflict as a chance to make it even, make it bigger, or make it different, then you will try to use a conflict situation to improve on whatever has been going on so far.

The make-it-even approach means dividing something even-steven so that both sides split whatever is being fought over right down the middle or dividing it in whatever way will make everybody feel like they got a good deal.

The make-it-bigger approach means that you figure out how to get more of whatever is being fought over. Not enough stuff to go around? Then work together to figure out how to get more stuff and divide it up.

The make-it-different approach means that you decide to work together on something other than whatever the fight was about at first. The fight may appear to be about one thing, for example, getting a fair share of stuff. A different look may show other possible causes. Maybe the whole thing concerns the way someone feels about conflict. It could concern the way someone feels about the way stuff has been divided up in the past or other deeper issues. In the make-it-different scenario, we find something different about the disagreement so that we can see it in a new way. For example, there may not be a way to get more stuff at the moment, but we may find out that both sides feel the same way about the way stuff has been divided up in the past.

When we make it different, we find solutions to the problem or we learn about one another by focusing on a part of the conflict that makes sense to everybody. We may not get more stuff when we look at how we have shared stuff in the past, but we may gain a better understanding of why we are fighting about stuff in the first place.

What Do I Think About Conflict Right Now?

Handout 1.7: Reflection Worksheet: What Do I Think About Conflict Right Now? is the first of a series of four reflection worksheets that you can use to think about what you are getting out of this workshop.

This workshop is designed to help you clarify your own points of view about conflict. The reflection sheets will help you organize everything you have been hearing, reading, and talking about up to that point. There is no need to tell anyone what is on your reflection sheet unless you want to. Reflection sheets are included to give you a chance to take a breath, slow down your brain, and examine old points of view or build new ones.

REFLECTION WORKSHEET: WHAT DO I THINK ABOUT CONFLICT RIGHT NOW?

Are there times when one side winning and another side losing is the only appropriate solution? When?

Can I think of three things that I will always fight for, no matter what?

What do most people fight about here at my company: ways of seeing, ways of knowing, ways of learning, ways of living, or ways of seeing conflict?

What are some other causes of conflict at my company?

RESPONSE

INTRODUCTION AND OBJECTIVES

Commentary: Tell participants that they will discuss different responses to conflict in this module: which ones work and which ones they think are "correct." Remind them again that you are not looking for a specific answer, but that it is their job as conflict experts to examine their own conclusions. (Remember that you are using the group's word for *conflict* throughout the workshop.)

Quickly review the objectives for this module:

 Facilitator: Refer participants to Handout 2.1: Module 2 Objectives.

- In this module you will examine what makes you respond the way that you do in conflict situations.
- You will think about whether conflict can be a positive thing for you, for other people, or for the company.
- You will think about whether you should change some of the ways you respond to conflict.

MODULE 2 OBJECTIVES

INTRODUCTION

What you think and feel about conflict can determine how you respond to it.

OBJECTIVES

- In this module you will examine what makes you respond the way that you do in conflict situations.
- You will think about whether conflict can be a positive thing for you, for other people, or for the company.
- You will think about whether you should change some of the ways you respond to conflict.

Remind the group of the *Bell Curve* exercise from the morning. Not everyone is entirely comfortable dealing with conflict. Sometimes we look for conflict, and sometimes conflict is thrust upon us.

 Discussion: Worthwhile Conflicts Ask the group for examples of worthwhile conflicts—conflicts that may not have been enjoyable but that needed to be engaged in because they were the right thing to do, or because of some good that came from them.

As people come up with examples, make certain that they explain briefly what made the conflict worthwhile. If the examples tend to be large and physically violent—wars and revolutions, for example—challenge participants to come up with local, everyday differences.

 Facilitator: Allow some discussion and disagreement about what is a worthwhile conflict, but understand that your job in the workshop is not to form consensus at this time. Your role is simply to ensure that all participants are heard, that they agree to disagree if necessary, and that they move on.

TRAINER Tip: Occasionally, a workshop group's word for conflict may seem to you to be a narrow choice. This section is a good place to test that view. For example, if the group chose *war* as its word for conflict, it might feel odd to you to use it to describe all conflicts. If you think that the word chosen by the group does not work for everyday use—for example, "I am having a war with my husband over how to fold towels"—ask the group the following: First, ask whether a statement like the one about towel folding sounds correct to them with their word in it. If so, continue to use it. If not, suggest the word *difference* as a general word, and tell them that you will all be revisiting the choice of a name for conflict at the end of the second day of the workshop. In the meantime, use the group's word whenever it works, and use *difference* only when absolutely necessary.

Commentary: Remind the group again that people are not always eager to engage in conflict.

 Facilitator: Refer the group to Handout 2.2: Reflection Worksheet: "Good" Conflict?

Individual Exercise: *"Good" Conflict?*

When participants have completed the "Good" Conflict? reflection worksheet, ask them to write down as many causes for willing participation in a conflict as they can think of by saying: "In the next three minutes, write down as many things as you can think of that would either draw you into a conflict or make you eager to join in a conflict."

Debriefing
After participants have finished, ask them: "So what makes conflict good?"
    Write their answers on a blank flip chart.
    Once you have written their answers to the question on a flipchart, create a fishbone diagram like the one in Flip Chart 2.1. In the "head" of the fish, write "So what makes conflict good?" The fish bones can be labeled "context," "approaches," "benefits," and "responses."

 Facilitator: Display Flip Chart 2.1: So What Makes Conflict Good?

Work with the group to assign their answers to the good conflict question to the various categories and list them on the fishbone diagram. Some responses may seem to fit into one or more categories, which is fine. If some responses fit on more than one "bone," go ahead and list them that way. Some may not fit into any category.
    If you need to create another category, draw and name another bone on the diagram with the group's help, and list their answers there.
    What you will create is a diagram—which is often messy—of some of the things that can make conflict a positive force. Once the diagram is finished, ask for someone in the group to sum up what it reveals.
    Ask for alternative explanations, or give one of your own. A simple summation could be: "It seems we have quite a few ideas about what can make conflict good." Follow up by explaining that it can be useful for us to have some idea about conflict as a positive whenever we need to decide how to respond to a particular conflict situation.

 TRAINER Tip: Remember to use the group's word for conflict!

REFLECTION WORKSHEET: "GOOD" CONFLICT?

Can you think of some conflicts that may have seemed uncomfortable or were unpleasant but produced good results?

Can you think of any conflicts that produced more good than they cost?

Can you think of any conflicts that people would be willing to go through again because of the good that came of them?

Can you think of a time here at our company when there was a difference between groups, individuals, or with a client or supplier and something good came out of facing it head on?

How could this have been handled to make it even better?

What makes it difficult to handle conflicts the way you just suggested?

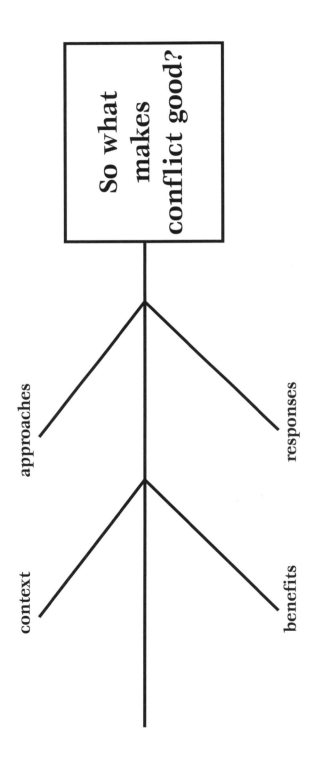

So what
makes
conflict good?

approaches

context

responses

benefits

👤👤👤 Group Activity: *Party Time*

Type
Role Play

Purpose
Many people have default responses to conflict, which are used whether they work or not. This exercise gives people a chance to disclose—at low personal risk—their usual approach to conflict so that they can examine what does or does not work for them.

Equipment Needed
- Flip-chart paper
- Markers for party symbols and slogans
- Handout 2.3: Party Descriptions
- Flip Chart 2.2: Party-Time Rules of Engagement

Preparation
Make copies of Handout 2.3: Party Descriptions and prepare Flip Chart 2.2: Party-Time Rules of Engagement.

Time
60 minutes

Introduction

 Facilitator: Distribute copies of Handout 2.3: Party Descriptions and go over them with participants.

Commentary: We have now done enough thinking and talking about conflict to take some general positions on how to handle it. Acknowledge that the group has also talked sufficiently about conflict to have more than one position to take.

Tell participants that just for fun you are going to let them create their own conflict party platforms, depending upon how they feel about conflict.

Instructions
Explain to participants that they will need to pick a party that best reflects how they prefer to deal with conflict.

Acknowledge that many people may have different approaches and that these approaches may even change in the midst of a particular conflict. What you are asking them to do for this exercise is to pick a party that best represents the approach they are most comfortable with. Some people may feel

PARTY DESCRIPTIONS

After reading over these brief descriptions, join the party that best matches the way you feel most comfortable when dealing with conflict.

- The Puzzle Party
  People in the Puzzle Party know that each conflict can be figured out if they approach it analytically and are dedicated to finding an answer.

- The Persuasion Party
  Persuasion Party members know that the best way to deal with conflict is to be sure that people see why it is in their best interest to adjust their positions and move on.

- The Palm Tree Party
  Palm trees can weather any storm. Palm Tree Party members know that if they bend enough, the conflict will pass over them. They may be shaken up when it is over, but they will survive.

- The Personal Party
  Personal Party people know that if they respect the other side and acknowledge their ideas and feelings (even if they disagree) the conflict will become secondary to what they learn about one another.

Party-Time Rules of Engagement

1. Opening Statement (2 min.)

2. Questions from the Floor (3 min.)

3. Closing Statement (2 min.)

comfortable in a particular party because they have been successful using that technique. Others may pick a party because it seems like the right thing to do. Still others may pick a party because they wish that was the way they approached conflict.

Symbols, Slogans, and Manifestos

Instructions

Ask participants to gather together into the party that best suits them. Ask them to design a party symbol and manifesto on a piece of flip-chart paper. They can also create a slogan for their party if they wish to do so. These slogans may take any form that the group chooses. Encourage them to be creative and to include all opinions. If there is a party that no one chooses to join, ask for volunteers to work on its manifesto and symbol for the sake of the exercise. If there are no takers, let it go.

Debate

Instructions

After the subgroups have completed their work, you will facilitate a debate among the groups. First, review Flip Chart 2.2: Party-Time Rules of Engagement and explain the following five steps:

1. Each group should select one or two presenters for the debate.
2. Each group will have a two-minute opening statement.
3. After all the opening statements are read, the floor will be open for questions. Each party will take turns fielding questions. That is, people can ask only one party questions for three minutes, then the next group gets its turn, and so on.
4. Finally, each party will make a two-minute closing statement.
5. Playful cheers, jeers, and other comments are allowed as long as kibitzers remain in their seats and the speakers are able to continue.

❓ Discussion

Debriefing
When the debate is finished, make the point that in any given situation, we may all use one or all of these strategies, sometimes one right after the other. Ask participants to drop their party affiliations and answer the following questions:

- When would the Personal Party approach help?
- When would the Palm Tree Party approach help?
- When would the Persuasion Party approach help?
- When would the Puzzle Party approach help?

Tell the group that most people do not stay loyal to only one party approach, but shift from one to the other, depending upon what is working or is appropriate to a changing situation.

Ask participants whether their experiences support that statement.

If you have time, ask for one or two examples from the participants' experiences when they have shifted strategies—for better or worse—in the middle of a conflict.

🧍 Individual Exercise: *How Can This Possibly Be Good for Me?*

Tell participants that they now have the opportunity to reflect on their work together up to this point.

Ask them to respond to the questions on Handout 2.4: Reflection Worksheet: How Can This Possibly Be Good for Me? Be sure that participants understand that their answers are for their eyes only, unless they decide to share them with the group or anyone else.

REFLECTION WORKSHEET: HOW CAN THIS POSSIBLY BE GOOD FOR ME?

As you think about and answer the questions on this reflection worksheet, think of a specific conflict situation at work that you have been a part of, will be a part of, should be a part of, or would like to be a part of.

WIIFM? *(What's in it for me?)*
What might I gain by being a part of this conflict?

What might I learn by being a part of this conflict?

What might change about me as a result of being a part of this conflict?

WIIFOP? *(What's in it for the other person?)*
What might the other person(s) gain because I am a part of this conflict?

WIIFU? *(What's in it for us?)*
What might everyone involved gain because I am a part of this conflict?

What might my team or department and I gain because I am a part of this conflict?

What might the company gain because I am a part of this conflict?

Can groups of people (teams, departments, or companies) learn from conflict? If they can, what can they learn?

So?
If there are benefits to conflict, should you wait for conflict to come to the surface by itself, or should you look for hidden conflict and intentionally bring it up?

What would you do if you decide to constructively leave conflict alone? What would you do if you decide to constructively bring conflict to the surface?

WRAP UP DAY ONE

Commentary: Thank the participants for their hard work, and for their patience with one another and with a process that may be strange to them. Congratulate them on what they have accomplished: They have talked and listened to one another and have clarified their own thinking about conflict.

Check each person's posted objective and place a check mark next to any that the participant in question agrees has been accomplished. An alternative is to ask each participant to check off his or her objective on the way out if he or she thinks it has been accomplished. You can start the second day of the workshop by reviewing the objectives that are checked off. If you find that only one or two are not checked off, you can talk about those and whether you expect to meet them.

Say that day two will cover planning and practicing what to do with what they have learned from one another.

Trainer Tip: A good wrap-up for day one or an opener for the second day is to ask everyone to write three to five things that they have learned or thought about in a new way so far. This can lead to a good review discussion. You can extend this exercise into the start of the second day by asking participants whether they have thought about doing anything differently as a result of the workshop so far.

Actions

REVIEW OF DAY ONE

Facilitator: It is a good idea to spend a few minutes reviewing what was learned on the first day of the workshop. This helps people to see the value they have derived from the workshop so far and gets them back into workshop mode for the second day.

INTRODUCTION AND OBJECTIVES

Commentary: It is now time to get down to the business of what to do about conflict. Remind participants that they have made expert decisions about how they prefer to deal with conflict and why.

Trainer Tip: Remember that you should be using the group's word for conflict as much as possible.

MODULE 3 OBJECTIVES

INTRODUCTION

We will now look at various ways of dealing with conflict. This will help us— as individuals and as a group—make decisions about how to handle conflicts here at work.

In this module, we will briefly review approaches to helping other people with their conflicts by acting as a neutral third party. We will also come to conclusions about what form of help is most appropriate at work.

OBJECTIVES

- You will test information about helping other people with their conflicts.
- You will have the opportunity to think about and discuss what types of help are best for you to offer when you are at work.
- You will make decisions about what you and the group should do about conflicts at work.

Facilitator: Refer participants to Handout 3.1: Module 3 Objectives

Introduce the following objectives:

- You will test information about helping other people with their conflicts.
- You will have the opportunity to think about and discuss what types of help are best for you to offer when you are at work.
- You will make decisions about what you and the group should do about conflicts at work.

Now, talk to the group about flexibility. Flexibility is a skill that can be learned and developed through practice. Often, conflict situations become stuck when the people involved refuse to try different approaches.

 Trainer Tip: Often, flexibility is a key part of your discussion at the end of the *Party Time* exercise. If that happens with your group, tie your comments on flexibility back to what they discovered in day one.

CONFLICT INTERVENTION

The following pages explore different types of conflict intervention.

Solving Problems

Commentary: One way to approach conflict is as a problem to be solved. Here, people put their heads together to figure out causes and solutions.

Remind the group of the stories *The Colored Ball* and *The Blind Men and the Elephant.* In *The Colored Ball,* progress could be made by people from each side going over to see the other side. This solution—taking the other person's perspective—is a great problem-solving solution. The solution of sitting and talking to each other, or sharing one another's experience, is a strategy that would help the blind men in the other story. Often, someone from outside the conflict is asked to help because she or he can bring a new perspective or look at the conflict as a problem to solve without emotion.

This outside party may be asked to decide for the people who have the conflict or may help them to sort it out. Tell participants that they will practice playing the part of the outside peacemaker.

Explain that there are many versions of third-party peacemakers in the world. Judges keep the peace, as do managers at work who make final decisions for people in a conflict. What we will be talking about are the third-party peacemakers who use their influence or the influence of the community to help make peace. We often call these people mediators. There are plenty of people who play this role in everyday life: bosses, parents, friends, clergy, and respected elders.

A mediator is usually someone who facilitates the activities between parties in a conflict. The mediator will sometimes make suggestions but is rarely expected to make a final decision. That is up to the people who own the conflict.

Ask participants whether they have examples from their individual cultures or experience about peacemaking by third parties.

 Facilitator: Refer participants to Handout 3.2: Looking Neutral.

After participants read Handout 3.2: Looking Neutral, ask for comments.

Practice Mediation

 **Group Activity:** *Two Siblings and One Orange—Take One*

Type
Demonstration

Purpose
Introduce a simple overview of two approaches to helping with other people's conflicts.

Equipment Needed
- Three chairs
- One table
- Paper
- Pencils or pens
- Scripts

Preparation
There are three ways to approach this exercise:

1. If your two workshop days are not consecutive, find two "hams" from the workshop, and have a quick meeting or two to rehearse before the next workshop day.

2. If your two workshop days are back-to-back, give the script to your volunteers at the end of day one. The main idea is for people to get a taste of the mediation process. Reassure your assistants that the performance is for fun and that you do not expect Academy Award performances.

LOOKING NEUTRAL

Sometimes we are asked to help someone who is in a conflict situation. We may be asked to take sides, or we may be asked to get in the middle as a neutral party to help sort things out.

Can we truly be neutral? To most of us, the word *neutral* means not taking sides. And we may be able to do that. We will still believe what we believe, and this may include an opinion about who is right and who is wrong.

When we decide not to take sides, we are neutral on the outside, but we still have our beliefs and points of view on the inside. That is, we "look" neutral.

Looking neutral might include not voicing an opinion, ensuring that everyone involved in the conflict is heard, and keeping people safe. We might look neutral by carefully choosing words so that they do not support one side or another. Looking neutral might also include keeping confidences—not telling the other side something that someone has told you in confidence.

Looking neutral is not dishonest. You are not going to stop being yourself while you help people with their differences. However, you are going to behave in a way that makes people feel sure that you will be as evenhanded as possible.

One way to be sure that you look neutral to the people you are trying to help is to check with them. When people ask you to help them as a neutral party, tell them what looking neutral looks like to you and see whether that works for them. If everybody can agree to what neutral looks like, you have a better picture of how you can help.

Here are some things to think about as you work on your own definition of what neutral looks like:

- What points of view do I have that might make it hard to look neutral?
  - Do I know something about the people or the situation that will make it hard for me to manage the way I react?
  - Do I know my hot buttons—things that can make me respond emotionally?
  - Do I have preconceived ideas about the people I have been asked to help?
  - Do I have preconceived ideas about the type of situation I have been asked to help with?

- What relationships or positions do I have that might make it hard to look neutral? Even as I work hard to be fair and look neutral, could somebody accuse me of having a conflict of interest?
  - Do I have a close friend or relative involved?
  - Does my job title or position make it difficult for me to look neutral?
  - Does any group I belong to make it hard for me to look neutral?
  - Is there a way to deal with these relationships or positions so that everyone feels I can still be of help?

- Are there any secrets I am not willing to keep?
  - What if someone tells me about a crime?
  - What if someone threatens violence?
  - What if someone breaks company policy?

- Is there a certain person or group that I feel usually needs to be protected from any other person or group?
  - Do I feel like I need to stick up for the underdog?
  - Do I need to defend company policy?

- If people come up with agreements or plans that I think are wrong or harmful, will I speak up?
  - If I think the plan won't work or won't last, should I say so?
  - If I think the plan is not fair to one side or the other, should I speak up?
  - If the plan involves dangerous or criminal activity, should I try to stop it?
  - Does the plan need to operate within company policy?

- Do I need to tell people my answers to these questions before I help them?

There are not necessarily right or wrong answers to any of these questions. The point is that the more you know about yourself and your point of view before deciding to look neutral, the better.

3. If you will be running this workshop several times, it may help to videotape this demonstration in advance and show it to the group. It is a break for you as a facilitator and can help break up the day for the participants.

Time
15 minutes

Commentary: This exercise is a demonstration piece so that the people in your workshop can see the most typical approach to mediation. It is meant to be lighthearted so that you can start the day in a nonintimidating, fun, and creative way.

To set up your demonstration of *Two Siblings and One Orange,* explain to the group that you will not be playing the role of the mother in *Two Sisters, One Orange* (Module 1). You will be mediating, that is, facilitating the meeting between the two siblings in such a way that they find their own solution. Although the mother's solution was a good one, the mediator works best when helping people find their own solutions. Sometimes it works and sometimes it does not.

Demonstrate the mediation process by showing the group an enactment of Handout 3.3: Two Siblings and One Orange—Take One: Problem-Solving Mediation Script.

TWO SIBLINGS AND ONE ORANGE— TAKE ONE: PROBLEM-SOLVING MEDIATION SCRIPT

People:

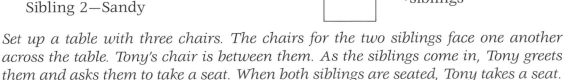

Mediator—Tony
Sibling 1—Jerry
Sibling 2—Sandy

Set up a table with three chairs. The chairs for the two siblings face one another across the table. Tony's chair is between them. As the siblings come in, Tony greets them and asks them to take a seat. When both siblings are seated, Tony takes a seat.

Tony: I understand that there is some problem about an orange between you two?

Jerry: I'll say! This jerk knows that I need the orange, and . . .

Sandy: *(interrupting)* That's exactly like Jerry! Everything is about what *Jerry* needs. . . .

Tony: *(interrupting)* Let's wait just a minute, Sandy. Jerry, you too. I need to tell you how this will work. Most important, you both need to know that I'm not here to make any decisions for you. This isn't like court where you tell me things and I decide for you. This is an opportunity for the two of you to sit down together, talk about what the problem is, and figure out a solution that works for both of you. How does that sound?

Jerry: I have a solution in mind already. We just have to get through to Simple Simon over there.

Tony: Right now I need to know that you are both willing to work together on this problem. You will get a chance to tell your story, Jerry. For now, tell me if you are willing to talk this out.

Jerry: Sure. I'll stay if Sandy stays.

Tony: Sandy?

Sandy: I'll stay, but Jerry has to stop calling me names.

Tony: Good. In fact, why don't we make that a ground rule for our meeting? "No name-calling."

The siblings nod their agreement.

Tony: Here's how this will work. Everything you tell me will be confidential. I won't tell anyone about what we talk about here unless you want me to. You may see me take notes so I can keep my thinking straight, but you'll also see me tear my notes up when we are finished. I won't take sides but will be here to be sure that you both are represented and to help you figure this out.

We'll start by having each of you bring me up to date on what the problem is. First one will speak and then the other. During that time, I don't want you to interrupt—just listen. If there is something you want to be sure to say, write it down and say it during your turn.

Once you have had your turns, we can ask questions and talk about different points of view. If we come up with a solution that works for both of you, we'll write it down and sign it.

Sound good?

Sandy and Jerry nod.

Tony: Who would like to go first?

Sandy: It may as well be Jerry. Jerry always goes first.

Jerry: All right, I will.

Tony: Is that really all right, Sandy?

Sandy: Yeah.

Jerry: Sandy has this self-image of being a great chef or something. I came home from running and wanted some fresh orange juice. It's full of antioxidants and vitamin C. I need it after a run, but—no! Sandy has to bake. I'm hot, I'm tired, I'm thirsty. So all I did was pick up the orange and start to walk out of the room. . . .

Sandy: I was using it!!!

Tony: *(calmly)* You'll get your turn, Sandy.

Jerry: See how Sandy always interrupts and yells? Anyway, I picked up the orange. . . .

Sandy: I do not interrupt and yell!

Tony: *(still calm, but a little more firmly)* Sandy, let's let Jerry finish. You may want to write down what you were going to say so you don't forget it.

(Sandy writes furiously on the tablet on the table: "I don't yell!!!")

Tony: Jerry?

Jerry: I picked up the orange and started to go out of the room and Sandy came after me screaming that the orange wasn't mine, that it was part of some recipe.

(There is a pause.)

Tony: Anything else, Jerry?

Jerry: That's about all there was to it. All I wanted was to make some orange juice.

Tony: Thanks. Now, Sandy, why don't you . . .

Sandy: I was using that orange! Jerry just waltzes in and grabs the orange without asking and I need the entire peel to grate into my special Blue Ribbon Pound Cake. It's just like Jerry to ignore what I need. It's not like Jerry isn't going to get any of the cake, but no! Jerry has to have juice. It's infuriating!

Tony: Anything else, Sandy?

Sandy: No.

Tony: Do you have questions for one another?

Jerry: Yeah. Why does Sandy have to be such a jerk?

Sandy: That's name-calling! You said you wouldn't call names!

Tony: We did agree to not call names, Jerry. Is there another way you can ask Sandy the question?

Jerry: Why is Sandy always acting like baking is the most important thing? Why can't I take the orange and make juice if I'm thirsty?

Tony: I don't know. Why don't you ask Sandy?

Sandy: I know that you want juice, but you want some of my Blue Ribbon Pound Cake, too. . . . If there's no orange peel, there's no Blue Ribbon Pound Cake. You just make me so mad when you come in and interrupt everything I have planned and take the orange just because you need juice. Blue Ribbon Pound Cakes don't grow on trees.

Jerry: You make great cakes, but when I come in all hot and thirsty, I really need my freshly squeezed orange juice. I can't wait to cut that orange open and squeeze the juice out of it.

Tony: Can you explain something to me? Sandy, how do you use the orange in your Blue Ribbon Pound Cake?

Sandy: I zest it.

Jerry: Oh, brother!

Sandy: That's what it's called. I have this thing like a little grater, and I rub it all over the orange peel and the peel comes off into the batter. It's what gives my Blue Ribbon Pound Cake that special something.

Tony: Thanks. And Jerry, how do you make juice?

Jerry: I cut the peel off and put the orange in the juicer.

Tony: Any ideas?

Sandy: Yes! If Jerry wants cake, then no juice for Jerry.

Jerry: That's just stupid. I'll make my juice, and you can dig the peel out of the trash for your stupid cake.

(There is a pause.)

Sandy: Better idea: I'll use the zest and when I'm done baking you can have the orange.

Jerry: I'm not waiting for you. When I come in I'm thirsty.

Tony: So what do we have so far? *(checks notes)* Sandy, you just need the peel, and Jerry, you just need the fruit.

Sandy: But I'm not digging the peel out of the trash.

Jerry: You wouldn't have to. I could leave it on the table for you. But I have to have my juice first.

Sandy: In other words, I have to wait for you to come back until I can finish my cake. This isn't working.

Tony: Wait a minute, Sandy. Is there some way that there could be juice ready when Jerry needed it and you wouldn't have to wait to start baking?

Sandy: I'm not making Jerry's juice, if that's what you mean.

Jerry: Just take the peel, and leave the fruit in the fridge. I'll make my own juice when I get home.

Tony: Will that work?

Sandy: Works for me.

Jerry: Will I still get some cake?

Discussion When the demonstration is finished, thank the two siblings and let them return to their regular seats.

Explain that the next steps in the process would often include writing an agreement for each sibling to sign: "The two siblings finally came to an agreement that worked for them about the orange. Were there any issues other than the orange that we could have talked about?"

Some groups will come up with answers to this; some will not. If your group has some answers, write them on a flip chart as they say them to you. If they do not, suggest that some other issues were brought up besides the orange, including:

- One calls the other names.
- Jerry always goes first.
- Jerry doesn't always seem to value Sandy's baking.
- Sandy yells and interrupts.
- Sandy says that Jerry ignores his or her needs.
- Sandy is very proud of the pound cake.
- At one point, Jerry says, "You make great cakes."
- Sandy and Jerry have slightly different values.

Explain that some or all of these things could help or hinder the success of the two siblings' agreement about the orange. Mediators need to decide what issues they should be focusing on.

 Facilitator: If you are following the two-day workshop script, you will now lead the Mediation Practice. If you do not have time for that, you can move right into the second demonstration, Two Siblings and One Orange— Take Two.

Tell the group that you will touch on the topic of looking for opportunities for personal growth while solving problems at a later time. For now, they will work on helping people solve their problems.

 Group Activity: *Mediation Practice*

Type
Role Play

Purpose
This exercise introduces the basics of third-party problem-solving mediation to group members. The exercise will not make instant mediators out of the people in your workshop. However, it will give participants the opportunity to try

on the role of mediator so that they can decide whether it is an approach worth pursuing in their organizations.

Equipment Needed
- Flip Chart 3.1: Mediation Practice Schedule
- Handout 3.4: Practice Case #1: Noise from Two Cubicles Down
- Handout 3.5: Practice Case #1: Noise from Two Cubicles Down: Notes for Lilly/Lyle
- Handout 3.6: Practice Case #1: Noise from Two Cubicles Down: Notes for Martin/Martha
- Handout 3.7: Practice Case #2: The Backup
- Handout 3.8: Practice Case #2: The Backup: Notes for Gina/Gene
- Handout 3.9: Practice Case #2: The Backup: Notes for Claude/Claudette
- Handout 3.10: Practice Case #3: Never Talk to Me That Way Again!
- Handout 3.11: Practice Case #3: Never Talk to Me That Way Again!: Notes for Tomás/Tammy
- Handout 3.12: Practice Case #3: Never Talk to Me That Way Again!: Notes for Leslie/Lorenzo
- Handout 3.13: Practice Case #4: My Old Friend Is My New Boss
- Handout 3.14: Practice Case #4: My Old Friend Is My New Boss: Notes for Doug/Dolores
- Handout 3.15: Practice Case #4: My Old Friend Is My New Boss: Notes for Kay/Ken
- Handout 3.16: Practice Case #5: R-E-S-P-E-C-T
- Handout 3.17: Practice Case #5: R-E-S-P-E-C-T: Notes for Paloma/Pete
- Handout 3.18: Practice Case #5: R-E-S-P-E-C-T: Notes for Hien/Hanna

Preparation
Prepare Flip Chart 3.1: Mediation Practice Schedule and make copies of handouts 3.4 through 3:18.

Time
2 hours, 45 minutes

Instructions
Divide participants into groups of three to five members each.

In each group, select one person to be the mediator and two people to be in conflict. The rest of the group will observe. Option: If the group is comfortable with less structured role playing, they may choose to use their examples from their *Two Sisters and One Orange* discussion instead of from the practice cases.

Walk the group through the schedule on Flip Chart 3.1: Mediation Practice Schedule as listed below. Inform participants that in real life a mediation meeting would take two or more hours, but that you will remind them of the time since this is only a practice. Go through each step in the schedule:

1. *Prep: Select case, select roles, read case.* Tell participants: Each mediator will have five minutes to review the cases in the Practice Cases section of your participant handouts. Choose which case you want to do, decide who will be taking what role, and read the case over quickly. Participants should read only the appropriate pages for their roles.

2. *Mediator: Greet participants.* Tell the mediator: To start the mediation, take no more than a minute to set the tone. The mediator should greet participants and ask them to be seated. The tone should be one of calm. Do not let anyone start in until the mediator has introduced the process.

3. *Mediator: Introduce the process.* The mediator should briefly explain the steps of the mediation process that are listed on the flip chart: introducing the process, turn taking, open exchange, identifying solutions, and writing the agreement. The mediator should tell the conflict participants that everything said in the meeting will be kept confidential unless they decide otherwise, and that the mediator will not be deciding the case the way a judge would but is there to help them to work things out. Check in with the participants from time to time to confirm that they understand you and that they are willing to go forward.

 Facilitator: Tell participants: This is a first practice, so don't be too hard on our mediators. You will be taking a turn at mediating soon, and you will need their help when it is your turn.

4. *Take turns.* Tell participants: First will be turn taking. Now each party has the opportunity to tell her or his story without interruption. If someone becomes excited and interrupts during turn taking, the mediator should firmly but gently remind him or her to write things down for later. Mediators should make notes throughout this step whenever a participant suggests a solution.

5. *Exchange openly.* Tell the mediator: When both sides have taken their turns, now is the time for participants to ask each other questions. Allow the participants to ask questions, argue, and interrupt. It is permissible during this period for people to get angry. Let participants wear themselves out. During the open exchange, the mediator should ask questions to help clarify what is being said or to help people understand each other. Listen carefully for phrases such as "What we should do is . . ." or "I agree . . ." or "I understand . . ." that may be useful in crafting solutions.

6. *Identify solutions.* The mediator should ask for ideas from the participants. Often, in a real mediation, you will know that the open exchange is over when people start introducing solutions without being prompted. Be careful that people are not introducing solutions too soon; that is, ensure that everyone has been heard before moving on to this step. If participants do not have any ideas, the mediator should look at the notes he or she has been jotting down for places where a solution was suggested. For example, the mediator could say, "Rudy said something a while ago about trying something new. Let's talk about that and see if it will work for both of you."

7. *Mediator: Write agreement.* Tell participants: If some or all of the solutions are agreeable to both participants, the mediator should write an agreement. There probably will not be sufficient time to write the entire agreement, but start one. Do not write like a lawyer. Use the participants' own words; for example: "Rudy and Morgan both agree that everyone will take turns playing horseshoes."

Facilitator: Keep track of the time. Tell participants when the time for each section has expired. Tell participants not to wait for time to be called if they are ready to move on. If they are not ready to move on when time is up, they should fast forward to the next section and pretend they are at the correct point. Remind everyone that this practice is merely to get a taste of the process.

8. *Mediator: Thank/praise the participants.* At the end of the session, the mediator should thank the participants for their hard work and praise them for trusting one another. The mediator should remind them that they can come back if they need help with this situation or any other in the future.

9. *Debrief as a group.* Participants should step out of their roles. Take five to ten minutes to talk about how it went. Go step-by-step through the process on the flip chart. What worked? What did not? How did it feel for the mediator? For the participants? Would you try this in real life?

10. *Begin again with new mediator.* Tell the group that when they are finished debriefing, it is the next person's turn to be the mediator. Let the participants know that you will keep track of time as they go through the exercise. The next mediator to practice may use the same case or choose a new one.

Facilitator: Tell participants to call you over if they get stuck or have any questions during the mediation.

Debriefing

After the mediation practice, ask for feedback. Call on each subgroup. First, ask the people in the conflict how they felt and if their problem was solved. Then ask for the observers to report. Finally, ask the mediator to talk about how it went and what could have been done differently.

Lead a discussion on what was learned. If the group needs prompting,

- Ask them whether they enjoyed it.
- Ask the mediators what worked and what did not work.
- Ask the disputants what worked and what did not work.
- Ask the group whether this is an approach that they would use in the future. Why or why not?

Mediation Practice Schedule

1. Prep: Select case, select roles, read case.   (3–5 min.)
2. Mediator: Greet participants.
3. Mediator: Introduce the process: (2–3 min.)
   a. Confidentiality
   b. "Looking neutral"
   c. Walk-through of the process
4. Take turns.   (±5 min. for each participant)
5. Exchange openly.   (5–7 min.)
6. Identify solutions.   (5–7 min.)
7. Mediator: Write agreement.   (3–5 min.)
8. Mediator: Thank/praise the participants.
9. Debrief as a group.   (5–10 min.)
10. Begin again with new mediator.

PRACTICE CASE #1:
NOISE FROM TWO CUBICLES DOWN

Lilly/Lyle and Martin/Martha are accounts receivable clerks. There are fifteen clerks in their department. All of them sit in cubicles and make calls reminding customers to submit payment.

In the six months that Lilly/Lyle has worked for the company, Lilly/Lyle has become the top bill collector in the department. Lilly/Lyle hits over 97 percent of Lilly's/Lyle's quota every month, while the department average is 92 percent. Martin/Martha has been in the department for three and a half years. Martin's/Martha's last review included praise for "your in-depth knowledge of the operation, your positive relationships with clients, and your professionalism."

Martin/Martha has a problem with Lilly/Lyle. Martin/Martha acknowledges that the other clerk gets results, but Lilly/Lyle tells jokes on the telephone and talks and laughs loudly. Martin/Martha finds this distracting. Martin's/Martha's approach with customers is quieter. Martin/Martha says that Lilly's/Lyle's lack of professionalism makes it hard to hear customers on the telephone.

"Sometimes," says Martin/Martha, "I can't even hear myself think."

Martin/Martha has talked with Lilly/Lyle about this on three separate occasions. Each time, Lilly/Lyle promised to be quieter. Martin/Martha says that Lilly/Lyle is quiet for a little while and then gets noisy again.

Lilly/Lyle is tired of Martin/Martha complaining about this. "I may be loud, but I get results."

Neither one of them wants to go to the manager about this. They are embarrassed about not being able to work it out. Besides, they do not want anyone to get in trouble.

Rita (or Ron), a friend from another department, recently attended a wonderful workshop called *The Conflict Management Skills Workshop*. Lilly/Lyle and Martin/Martha have asked Rita/Ron to help them work things out.

PRACTICE CASE #1:
NOISE FROM TWO CUBICLES DOWN

Notes for Lilly/Lyle

You have been in the department for only six months and already you are the best collector the company has. For five of the six months, you have outperformed the department average by at least 5 percent.

You love your job and are proud of your success. The manager has told you that you have potential to move up in the company. "People have their eyes on you," were her exact words.

Although you have no accounting background, you are smart and can figure out most jobs. Your partner is a dentist, and you worked part-time in the dental practice as office manager. In fact, your current boss offered you a job after overhearing a collections call you made in the dentist's office. When you came to work, the manager said you were a natural and didn't need any training. "Here's your portfolio. I'm turning you loose," was all the manager ever said.

You feel that it would be inappropriate to mention to anyone else that you may be in line for a promotion. Although you want to get along with Martin/Martha, you will never do anything that might lower your productivity. You think Martin/Martha may be jealous of your success.

PRACTICE CASE #1: NOISE FROM TWO CUBICLES DOWN

Notes for Martin/Martha

The last thing you want in the world is to have problems with anybody at work. You are usually very quiet and keep to yourself. You wouldn't even have spoken with Lilly/Lyle about this, except that it is very important to you.

In your three and a half years in the department, you have trained several people. You are pleased that one of your trainees has been promoted into management and another is doing well in payables. "At the end of the day," you tell your trainees, "the company lives or dies in accounts receivable."

Lilly/Lyle is the only new hire you haven't trained in more than two years. The other new hires usually came from business school or had some accounting or bookkeeping training. The only prior experience Lilly/Lyle had was working in a family dental practice as office manager. The manager said that she had seen Lilly/Lyle in action and that no training was necessary. "Here's your portfolio. I'm turning you loose," was all the manager ever said.

You are afraid that Lilly's/Lyle's success is beginner's luck, and that other new people will adopt the same loud, rambunctious style. You are also afraid that your numbers might start slipping. It is getting harder and harder to concentrate with all that noise coming from two cubicles down.

PRACTICE CASE #2: THE BACKUP

Gina/Gene has been the only drill press operator on the third shift for seventeen years. Nobody ever needs to tell Gina/Gene what to do. As Gina/Gene says, "The work is there. The work gets done."

Over the years, Gina/Gene has become sort of a one-person department. Gina/Gene is always on time but takes breaks depending on the work flow. If it's a busy night, Gina/Gene works right through the break. If things are slow, Gina/Gene will go out on the loading dock for a smoke. "It all evens out in the end," says Gina/Gene.

Two weeks ago, the supervisor brought Claude/Claudette over to the drill press. Claude/Claudette, the supervisor said, is the new backup drill press operator. "In case we get busy or you get sick or something."

It is Gina's/Gene's responsibility to train Claude/Claudette. Claude/Claudette has been trained on newer equipment, but the old machine that Gina/Gene runs has its quirks.

At first Gina/Gene got along well with the new trainee. It was nice to have someone to talk to. The problem, according to Gina/Gene, is that there is only one workstation and there isn't enough to keep two people busy. So, while Claude/Claudette is running the drill press, Gina/Gene does setup work. When the setup work is done, Gina/Gene stands near the machine and makes comments on Claude's/Claudette's work.

Claude/Claudette is annoyed by this behavior. Gina/Gene has said that Claude/Claudette is doing a fine job but seems to feel that there is still a need to comment on everything the other worker does.

The supervisor insists that these two work together. He has sent them to Ted/Tania in human resources. Ted/Tania recently attended a workshop where they practiced problem solving and thinks this method might help the two drill press operators.

PRACTICE CASE #2: THE BACKUP

Notes for Gina/Gene

You have worked third shift longer than anyone in the company. For seventeen years, you have run the drill press. Nobody can remember when anyone else has run that machine on graveyard. Everyone calls it Gina's/Gene's Machine.

You don't need supervision. You are used to setting your own pace and proud of the high-quality work that you put out. In the seventeen years you have run your machine, you have missed only eight days of work. One year, your picture was in the company's annual report. Your coworkers had the picture framed, and it is hanging on a post near your machine.

You can't see why they wanted to train a backup, but you just decided to "keep quiet and do what I was told." Claude/Claudette is a nice person and picked up the quirks of the old machine very quickly.

After about three weeks, there was no more need for training, but you still keep an eye on things. Once, several of Claude's/Claudette's pieces went out with a glaring mistake. The work was kicked back to your station. You feel that it reflected badly on you.

You know it bothers Claude/Claudette to have you watching all the time, but you aren't going to get into trouble because of someone else's mistakes.

Last week Claude/Claudette yelled at you to back off. You muttered an obscenity, and Claude/Claudette went to the supervisor. Now you have to go to a meeting in human resources to talk things out.

You don't know why there has to be a meeting, but you have decided to "keep quiet and do what I am told."

PRACTICE CASE #2: THE BACKUP

Notes for Claude/Claudette

Gina/Gene is driving you nuts. You feel like you can barely breathe the way Gina/Gene hovers while you work.

Gina/Gene has said that you run the drill press as well as anybody, but because of one time when you misread a work order, you can't get any peace. The work was sent back and you fixed it, but Gina/Gene continues to bring it up.

You like the job. The work is easy. When Gina/Gene is running the drill press, you sweep and do setup work. You used to read when things were really slow, but lately—just so Gina/Gene can see how it feels—you have been standing and watching while Gina/Gene works.

You are convinced that this has caused Gina/Gene to stand even closer to your machine while you are working. Last week, you lost your temper and yelled, "Get out of my face!"

You know that wasn't the correct way to handle things, but Gina/Gene made things even worse by cursing at you. You don't need to take that from anyone, so you told the supervisor.

Now the supervisor has told you that if you don't work things out, he will find someone who can. You are going to meet with Ted/Tania in human resources.

PRACTICE CASE #3: NEVER TALK TO ME THAT WAY AGAIN!

Leslie/Lorenzo is the vice president of sales for HowdyCard, a greeting card company. Tomás/Tammy heads up human resources. They have never seemed to get along very well.

None of Leslie's/Lorenzo's people have ever gone through Tomás's/Tammy's orientation program, and the only time they speak to one another is if there is a compensation question for one of the salespeople.

Tomás/Tammy presented a graph at the last executive council meeting that showed the percentage of compliance for attendance at the orientation program. The sales department was highlighted in brilliant red ink, as was the chart's title: "Zero Cooperation from Sales."

There was an uncomfortable pause when the slide went up. Finally, Leslie/Lorenzo said, "I guess we were too busy having HowdyCard's best year ever to slow down and sit through orientation."

"A little cooperation would go a long way," countered Tomás/Tammy. "Everyone is tired of the arrogance of the salespeople. It's as if rules apply to everyone but them."

"Hey," said Leslie/Lorenzo, "the rule is that training programs are discretionary by department. Maybe if the orientation weren't so boring, people would want to go to it without me putting a gun to their head. Anyway, salespeople would rather be making money than wasting it."

Now Tomás/Tammy was really angry. "It's people like you who will keep this company from ever moving beyond the status quo."

Leslie/Lorenzo sat quietly and seethed for a moment, then said, "That's it," and left the meeting.

Tomás/Tammy has asked Barry/Beryl, a business professor at the local community college, to help them work this out. After several tries, Barry/Beryl reached Leslie/Lorenzo on the telephone.

"I'll come to the meeting," said Leslie/Lorenzo, "but Tomás/Tammy can never talk to me that way again."

PRACTICE CASE #3:
NEVER TALK TO ME THAT WAY AGAIN!

Notes for Tomás/Tammy

As head of human resources at HowdyCard, you have worked hard to make important changes in the company. Your new-hire orientation program has helped people to feel comfortable as they start work in the hectic and creative atmosphere of the greeting card business. You are convinced that this program is a major reason why employee attrition is at an all-time low.

You had to sell the orientation program to your colleagues over a period of one year. At first, nobody would listen. When you started receiving rave reviews for the program, people started attending one department at a time.

Now people don't know what they did without the program. It is a major feather in your cap.

You are offended that Leslie/Lorenzo and the sales department don't take the services that your group provides more seriously. You are also worried that sales will become out of step with the culture of the company. This could cause factions to form.

Leslie/Lorenzo never even responded to your message to meet about orientation. The sales group also goes around your department and does its own recruiting. The last straw for you was when Leslie/Lorenzo went outside of the company for sales training even though your training manager was formerly the sales trainer at your biggest competitor.

PRACTICE CASE #3:
NEVER TALK TO ME THAT WAY AGAIN!

Notes for Leslie/Lorenzo

You have been heading up sales for HowdyCard for three years. Sales numbers have increased by more than 35 percent for each year that you have been at the helm. You use your instincts to make hiring and other business decisions, and you don't want human resources to get in the way of your or the company's success.

You keep meetings and training to a minimum and it is working well for you. You tell your salespeople, "If you aren't selling, you're not making money for yourself or the company. If you're not making money for yourself, why are you coming to work? If you're not making money for the company, why are we letting you come to work?"

You want human resources out of your hair. You even sent some of your people to an outside training class even though you know the training manager of the human resources department used to do sales training for your biggest competitor.

The only reason you have agreed to meet with Tomás/Tammy and Barry/Beryl is that you think you may have overly avoided training classes and that you may start looking uncooperative in the eyes of the CEO.

You would be willing to give training a try if it could be scheduled around the busy days of your salespeople, but you aren't going to even talk to Tomás/Tammy at the meeting unless you hear a sincere apology.

PRACTICE CASE #4: MY OLD FRIEND IS MY NEW BOSS

Doug/Dolores and Kay/Ken have worked at the jewelry counter at York's Department Store since graduating from high school four years ago. They did not know one another very well in high school, but during the time they have worked together, they have become good friends. They are both on the company softball team and sometimes get together outside of work.

Last week the section manager, Xina Henderson, quit. Both Doug/Dolores and Kay/Ken applied for Xina's job. The operations manager said it was a tough decision between two good workers, but he picked Doug/Dolores. What influenced the choice the most, he said, was that Doug/Dolores has been attending college business classes on Wednesday nights.

The manager told Kay/Ken, "If you want to get ahead, you should take a page out of Doug's/Dolores's book."

Kay/Ken is working the jewelry counter alone until Doug/Dolores finds a replacement. Kay/Ken was late for work on Doug's/Dolores's first day as section manager. In the past, if one of the two friends was late, the other one would work alone to set up the register and the displays in time for opening. When the first customers arrived that particular morning, the jewelry counter was not ready for business.

Doug/Dolores told Kay/Ken that lateness is unacceptable even though they are friends. Doug/Dolores stopped by the jewelry counter before Kay's/Ken's lunch break to see if they could eat together. Kay/Ken said, "There's nothing that says I have to eat with the boss."

Since then, the two friends have spoken only when they had to. Kay/Ken has started to call in sick every Monday. Doug/Dolores is worried that the excessive absences may get Kay/Ken in trouble and stopped by to talk about it. Doug/Dolores said, "If you've got a problem, boss, write me up."

Nguyen/Nora, who works in the cafeteria, has just finished a workshop called *The Conflict Management Skills Workshop*. After listening to Kay/Ken complain about Doug/Dolores, Nguyen/Nora has convinced the two friends to sit down together to try to work things out. They have agreed to meet in the training room after closing.

PRACTICE CASE #4:
MY OLD FRIEND IS MY NEW BOSS

Notes for Doug/Dolores

Kay/Ken is your best friend. You are worried because Kay/Ken is nearly out of sick days, and you may have to do a write-up if these Monday absences continue. The absences also add to your workload and make you look bad to your boss. This makes you angry. You expected better performance from your friend.

You think one thing that is bothering Kay/Ken is that you were both planning on buying a Jet Ski together until you decided to spend money to go to night classes.

You had a brief argument about the Jet Ski, and you thought it was over. Now the manager has made a big deal out of you being promoted instead of Kay/Ken because you are taking classes. You are certain this has added fuel to the fire.

PRACTICE CASE #4:
MY OLD FRIEND IS MY NEW BOSS

Notes for Kay/Ken

Doug/Dolores is your best friend. In the old days, you would cover for one another. Now you feel that Doug/Dolores is going by the book too much.

You are angry and feel like your friend has abandoned you. Last year, the two of you saved up to buy a Jet Ski together, and then Doug/Dolores decided to spend money on night classes instead.

Now the manager can't stop talking about how Doug/Dolores is leadership material because of the classes.

You came in late on Doug's/Dolores's first day and things have gone downhill since then. You don't want to lose your friend or your job, but you don't know what to do. You have been looking at the help-wanted advertisements on Sundays and calling in sick on Mondays so that you can go to interviews. You're afraid that if the "new" Doug/Dolores finds out, you will be fired.

PRACTICE CASE #5:
R-E-S-P-E-C-T

Hien/Hanna and Paloma/Pete work together at the Crown Cab & Limo Co. dispatch office. Paloma/Pete supervises Hien/Hanna and two other dispatchers. Crown Cab has a regular street cab service and also rents limousines.

Recently, the company has begun chartering buses to pick up large groups of convention goers at the airport. The company not only provides the buses but also has a crew of greeters who hold up signs for the incoming clients and direct them through baggage claim and onto the buses. A large meeting may have more than a thousand people arriving during a twelve-hour period.

When the company has a convention coming into town, Paloma/Pete goes to the airport to supervise the greeters and to ensure that everything goes smoothly. In Paloma/Pete's absence, Hien/Hanna takes over supervisory duties at dispatch.

Paloma/Pete is worried that the new supervisor duties may be too much for Hien/Hanna to handle. Hien/Hanna seems curt when talking to drivers, and the other two dispatchers complain that Hien/Hanna yells at them.

Paloma/Pete asked Hien/Hanna about this change in behavior. Hien/Hanna said, "I'm tired of the way you disrespect me and continually undermine my authority." Paloma/Pete doesn't understand what Hien/Hanna is talking about but is afraid to talk about it further because Hien/Hanna has a reputation for yelling when angry.

"I can put up with a lot," says Paloma/Pete, "but if Hien/Hanna yells at me, I know I'm going to lose my temper."

Crown Cab is two doors down from the community mediation center. Paloma/Pete asked Olga/Omar from the center to see whether Hien/Hanna would agree to a meeting.

"I think it's a waste of time," says Hien/Hanna, "but I'll try anything to make working with Paloma/Pete better."

PRACTICE CASE #5: R-E-S-P-E-C-T

Notes for Paloma/Pete

You work hard and you are tired. The company is growing and you now have to not only run the dispatch office, but you supervise the new airport crews as well. You enjoy the excitement and the pressure to some extent, but there are downsides. You don't feel as if your salary has kept up with your responsibilities. You also have an eight-year-old daughter who usually stays with you every other weekend. You have missed the last two weekends. You feel as if you are not being a very good parent, and your ex is beginning to lose patience.

Now on top of all this, Hien/Hanna is acting strangely. You don't know whether it is the pressure, but this usually outstanding worker is complaining to everyone who will listen that you are somehow disrespectful.

On your way past Hien's/Hanna's desk the other day, you asked what the problem is. Hien/Hanna said, "I'm tired of the way you disrespect me and continually undermine my authority."

You were in a hurry to get to the airport, and you didn't want to start an argument, so you left without saying anything more. You have asked Olga/Omar, a volunteer at the local community mediation center, to help. Hien/Hanna has reluctantly agreed to come to a meeting.

PRACTICE CASE #5:
R-E-S-P-E-C-T

Notes for Hien/Hanna

You work hard as a dispatcher and you are tired. The company is growing and you now have the added responsibility of supervising the other dispatchers when Paloma/Pete is away.

You enjoy the excitement and the pressure to some extent, but there are downsides. You don't feel like your salary has kept up with your responsibilities. You also like to work out at the gym three evenings a week and play in an adult soccer league on Saturdays. Lately, your work schedule has been keeping you away from the gym. Last Saturday, you were late for a match. You are afraid that if you start missing soccer matches and practices, the coach may ask you to step aside for another player.

Now on top of all this, Paloma/Pete is acting strangely. You don't know whether it is the pressure, but you used to like this boss. Now suddenly, you are being treated with disrespect. Paloma/Pete shouts incomplete instructions at you on the way out the door. If you don't get the instructions right, Paloma/Pete corrects you in front of everybody else.

As if this weren't bad enough, when you give the other dispatchers instructions, they often will not follow them. A typical response is, "That's not what Paloma/Pete told me to do." How can you possibly supervise the dispatchers without Paloma's/Pete's support?

Paloma/Pete and somebody from the community mediation center have asked you to come to a meeting. You don't think anyone can get through to Paloma/Pete, but you decide to go if it will help to keep the peace.

TRANSFORMATIVE MEDIATION

Commentary: There are some mediators who see their role not as problem solver but as a person who helps people in conflict to learn and grow from the experience. This approach was introduced by Robert A. Baruch Bush and Joseph P. Folger in their book, *The Promise of Mediation* (Jossey-Bass, 1994). Bush and Folger call what they teach *transformative mediation.* In transformative mediation, the mediator looks for opportunities for empowerment and recognition. Empowerment occurs when people realize that they have the power to deal with their own conflicts and to speak out in their own voice about what they need. Recognition is the acknowledgment of the other person's feelings, rights, and empowerment. Recognition does not necessarily mean that you agree with the other person, but that you recognize him or her as an individual, not as a piece of the puzzle to be solved.

The next exercise is the follow-up exercise for *Two Siblings and One Orange—Take One.* As with *Two Siblings and One Orange—Take One,* this exercise is a demonstration piece so that the people in your workshop can see the most typical approach to mediation. It is meant to be lighthearted so that you can start the day in a nonintimidating, fun, and creative way.

👤👤👤 Group Activity: *Two Siblings and One Orange— Take Two*

Type
Demonstration

Purpose
Introduce a simple overview of the transformative approach to helping with other people's conflicts.

Equipment Needed
- Three chairs
- One table
- Paper
- Pencils or pens
- Handout 3.19: Two Siblings and One Orange—Take Two: Transformative Mediation Script

Preparation
Make copies of Handout 3.19: Two Siblings and One Orange—Take Two: Transformative Mediation Script.

There are three ways to approach this exercise:

1. If your two workshop days are not consecutive, find two "hams" from the workshop, and have a quick meeting or two to rehearse before the next workshop day.

2. If your two workshop days are back-to-back, give the script to your volunteers at the end of day one. The main idea is for people to get a taste of the mediation process. Reassure your helpers that the performance is for fun and that you do not expect Academy Award performances.

3. If you will be running this workshop several times, it may help to videotape this demonstration in advance and show it to the group. It is a break for you as a facilitator and can help break up the day for the participants.

Time
5 minutes

Be sure to make the point that solving the problem is sometimes a result of the transformative model, but that the emphasis is on allowing people to discover and develop the skills and attitudes that will help them to live better with one another.

Ask the participants if they saw any difference between the ways the mediator worked in the first and second versions of Sandy and Jerry's meeting about the orange. This can be hard to see sometimes. If the group needs help, explain that in the second example the mediator did not really focus on how to solve the orange problem. The second time around the focus was on helping Sandy and Jerry to see each other's needs. It was most important that each of them could talk about what they needed for themselves.

In the first example, the meeting was about solving the problem of the orange. If an idea for a solution came up, the mediator helped Sandy and Jerry to zero in on it. Then they would talk through whether or not it might work for them. In the second meeting the mediator started by asking Jerry and Sandy what the issue was. This meeting was more of a conversation about their relationship with one another.

The first example, problem solving, ended with a truce that let Sandy and Jerry split the orange. The transformative mediator in the second example listened for ways to help Sandy hear what was important to Jerry and vice versa. The transformative mediator's goal is to help people understand that they can work through their own problems while seeing the importance and value of the other person's point of view. In the second example, Jerry and Sandy learned about themselves and each other. This gave them a good chance not only of figuring out what to do about the orange, but also of how to deal with other conflicts in the future.

How Deep Is Too Deep?

Tell the group that many people feel that it is important to go beyond the surface issues to help people in a conflict situation. Would the two siblings' orange problem be solved in the long term if they did not improve how they talked with one another? Some other issues that may be important are the relationships between the two people, individual feelings of personal ability, or the need to feel in control of one's future.

TWO SIBLINGS AND ONE ORANGE—
TAKE TWO: TRANSFORMATIVE
MEDIATION SCRIPT

People:

> Mediator—Tony
> Sibling 1—Jerry
> Sibling 2—Sandy

A table and several chairs are available. As the siblings come in, Tony greets them and asks them to take a seat. They sit where they choose. When both siblings are seated, Tony takes a seat.

Tony: How can I help you?

Jerry: We're here because of Sandy. We have one orange in the house. This jerk knows that I need it, and . . .

Sandy: *(interrupting)* That's exactly like Jerry! Everything is about what *Jerry* needs. . . .

Jerry: Will you listen to this hysteria! It should be pretty easy for you to figure out what we need to do here.

Tony: *(interrupting)* Let's wait just a minute, Jerry. Sandy, you too. You need to figure out how I can help you with this. I'm not here to make any decisions for you. This isn't like court where you tell me things and I decide for you. This is an opportunity for the two of you to sit down together, and really listen to one another as you talk about what's going on with the orange. How does that sound?

Jerry: I have a solution in mind already. We just have to get through to Simple Simon over there.

Tony: Right now I need to know that you are both willing to listen to one another. For now, tell me if you are willing to talk this out.

Jerry: Sure. I'll stay if Sandy stays.

Tony: Sandy?

Sandy: I'll stay, but Jerry has to stop calling me Simple Simon.

Tony: Does that work for you, Jerry?

Jerry: Sure.

Tony: Okay. *(writing)* "Jerry won't call Sandy Simple Simon."

Sandy: Or any other name!

Tony: Shall we make that a rule for going forward?

The siblings nod their agreement.

Tony: How does this sound? Everything you tell me will be confidential. I won't tell anyone about what we talk about here unless you want me to. You may see me take notes so I can keep my thinking straight, but you'll also see me tear my notes up when we are finished. I won't take sides but will be here to be sure that you both are represented and to help you find out what is truly important to one another. Sound good?

Sandy and Jerry nod.

Tony: Who would like to go first?

Sandy: It may as well be Jerry. Jerry always goes first.

Jerry: All right, I will.

Tony: Is that really all right, Sandy?

Sandy: Yeah.

Jerry: Sandy has this self-image of being a great chef or something. I came home from running and wanted some fresh orange juice. It's full of antioxidants and vitamin C. I need it after a run, but—no! Sandy has to bake. I'm hot, I'm tired, I'm thirsty. So all I did was pick up the orange and start to walk out of the room. . . .

Sandy: I was using it!

Jerry: See how Sandy always interrupts and yells? Anyway, I picked up the orange. . . .

Sandy: I do not interrupt and yell!

Tony: Jerry?

Jerry: I picked up the orange and started to go out of the room and Sandy came after me screaming that the orange wasn't mine, that it was part of some recipe.

(There is a pause.)

Tony: Anything else, Jerry?

Jerry: That's about all there was to it. All I wanted was to make some orange juice.

Sandy: I was using that orange! Jerry just waltzes in and grabs the orange without asking, and I need the entire peel to grate into my special Blue Ribbon Pound Cake. It's just like Jerry to ignore what I need. It's not like Jerry isn't going to get any of the cake, but no! Jerry has to have juice. It's infuriating!

Tony: Anything else, Sandy?

Sandy: No.

Tony: Do you have questions for one another?

Jerry: Yeah. Why does Sandy have to be such a jerk?

Sandy: That's name-calling! You said you wouldn't call names!

Tony: We did agree to not call names, Jerry. Is there another way you can ask Sandy the question?

Jerry: Why is Sandy always acting like baking is the most important thing? Why can't I take the orange and make juice if I'm thirsty?

Tony: I don't know. Why don't you ask Sandy?

Sandy: I know that you want juice, but you want some of my Blue Ribbon Pound Cake, too. . . . If there's no orange peel, there's no Blue Ribbon Pound Cake. You just make me so mad when you come in and interrupt everything I have planned and take the orange just because you need juice. Blue Ribbon Pound Cakes don't grow on trees.

Jerry: You make great cakes, but when I come in all hot and thirsty, I really need my freshly squeezed orange juice. I can't wait to cut that orange open and squeeze the juice out of it.

Tony: Sandy, I think that Jerry has said something that you may want to hear. Jerry, what do you think about Sandy's cakes?

Jerry: I think they're great. You can be a real pain, sometimes, but your cakes are the best.

Sandy: Then, why can't you let me use the orange when I need it?

Tony: Please wait, Sandy. Did you hear Jerry talk about your baking?

Sandy: What?

Tony: Jerry?

Jerry: You're an excellent baker.

Sandy: Wow. Thanks. You always seem to be making fun of my baking. If you like my baking so much, why couldn't you see that I needed the orange?

Jerry: I didn't know you needed the orange. I really needed orange juice after my run. You know the electrolytes . . .

Sandy: Right. And the vitamin C.

Jerry: That's right. And the vitamin C. This is very important to me.

Sandy: I know.

There is an uncomfortable silence.

Tony: What else?

Jerry: Sometimes Sandy gets excited and interrupts, but it's really not a problem.

Tony: It doesn't bother you?

Jerry: Well, yes, but I know that when I get excited I call Sandy Simple Simon.

Sandy: That has to stop, no matter what.

Jerry: I'll be more careful.

Sandy: More careful might not be good enough. It really bothers me when you call me names.

Jerry: Well, then don't be so stupid about whether or not I can make orange juice.

Sandy: Well, maybe you should open your eyes and see that I'm baking and I have everything laid out that I need. Everything—including the only orange in the house.

Jerry: I can't read your mind, Sandy!

Sandy: You know how I bake. Just pay attention once in a while and you would know that if an orange is on the counter with all of my stuff, I'm going to use it. All you think about is what you need at the moment.

Jerry: Well, all you think about is what you need to bake your stupid cakes!

Tony: Jerry, what do you think about Sandy's baking?

Jerry: I know. Sandy's cakes are great. I meant that. But there are other things in life.

Tony: Can you think of a way to tell Sandy what you mean without starting a fight?

Jerry: *(after a pause)* Not really.

Tony: Sandy, what would work for you?

Sandy: I think Jerry likes my cakes but thinks that's all I have in my life. Jerry is wrong. There are many things about me that people don't know.

Jerry: I know what you mean. Sometimes people say that all I do is run.

The questions that people who want to help with other people's business should ask themselves are: How deep is too deep? When does helping become meddling? When are we in over our heads?

Explain that people who teach and write books and articles about conflict often disagree about what the job of a helper should be.

 **Group Activity:** *How Deep Is Too Deep?*

Type
Reflection and Discussion

Purpose
Now that the people in your workshop have spent time talking about and reflecting on different approaches to conflict, this exercise gives them a chance to think about what types and levels of help are appropriate if people ask for help with their workplace conflicts.

Equipment Needed
- Flip Chart 3.2: How Deep Is Too Deep?
- Markers

Preparation
Draw Flip Chart 3.2: How Deep Is Too Deep?

Time
30 minutes

Instructions
Show Flip Chart 3.2: How Deep Is Too Deep? to the group.

 Trainer Tip: For a briefer exercise, you may choose to use only a few of the flip-chart items. You may also create some of your own that are relevant to your workplace.

Commentary: Tell participants that these are a few of the hot topics used for helping people to resolve their conflicts. The last two days have been spent sorting through different ideas about conflict. Now every person in the group can think about where he or she stands on the question "how deep is too deep?" when it comes to helping other people with their conflicts.

Instructions

Using the commentary on the pages accompanying the sample flip chart, explain each item on the chart. At the end of each explanation, ask for a show of hands as to whether the approach is too deep, about right, or not deep enough for helping people with their conflicts at work.

Stress to participants that they are talking specifically about helping with conflict at work. Mark the number of votes for each response on the chart. Some people may want to talk about some of the items on the flip chart.

How Deep Is Too Deep?

	Too Deep	About Right	Not Deep Enough
1. Help communicate better.			
2. Solve the problem and move on.			
3. Help learn about respect.			
4. Help with contributing feelings.			
5. Help with conflicting beliefs.			
6. Help understand cultural differences.			
7. Help people see response patterns.			

continued

	Too Deep	About Right	Not Deep Enough
8. Help people see others' points of view.			
9. Help people choose words.			
10. Balance power.			
11. Coach better listening.			
12. Help acknowledge others' needs.			
13. Help find common ground.			
14. Let people be upset.			
15. Help people change the system.			

continued

	Too Deep	About Right	Not Deep Enough
16. Let people not fix it.			
17. Be sure they talk about real issues.			
18. Stick up for the underdog.			
19. Make experts.			
20. Stop lawsuits.			
21. Settle once and for all.			
22. Convert.			

Commentary:

1. *Help communicate better.* Some people think that if we are going to help, we need to teach people communication skills, or at least help them figure out how to communicate better in specific situations.

2. *Solve the problem and move on.* In the example of Rueben and Laurel, the two people who had an office space problem, the mediator's focus would be on helping them to work out a solution. It wouldn't matter whether it was building a new office, drafting a sharing arrangement, or creating some other setup. Once agreement was reached on how to move forward, it would be back to work for all concerned. The goal is to solve the problem without getting into issues of rights, respect, or self-image.

3. *Help learn about respect.* Some helpers believe that besides solving the problem, people need to view conflict as an opportunity to learn about having and showing respect for the other person.

4. *Help with contributing feelings.* We all know that behind many conflicts there are complicated feelings. Is it the helper's job to encourage people to explore their feelings?

5. *Help with conflicting beliefs.* Is it the helper's job to encourage people to examine what lies behind their beliefs?

6. *Help understand cultural differences.* Do we teach about or point out cultural differences that may be contributing to the conflict?

7. *Help people see response patterns.* Should the helper point out response patterns—those automatic reactions that people have in conflict situations—as a way of encouraging people to consider changing their behavior?

8. *Help people see others' points of view.* Should we work to help people discover the validity of, or at least the origins of, the other side's point of view?

9. *Help people choose words.* Should the helper challenge participants to choose language that will help the other person hear them better?

10. *Balance power.* Often, conflicts come up between people who have different amounts of power in society, at work, or in some other relationship. Should a helper try to balance this out? For example, in a dispute between a supervisor and her employee, should the helper let the employee talk first or longer, sit on the employee's side of the table to make him feel safer, outnumber the supervisor by having more employees in the room than supervisors, or interrupt if the supervisor begins to remind the employee who is boss?

11. *Coach better listening.* Some people who help with conflicts think it is a good idea to train people on listening and other constructive communication skills before they actually start working with the other side. Is this a good idea?

12. *Help acknowledge others' needs.* Should a helper point out one side's needs to the other side as they come up?

13. *Help find common ground.* Should we either point out or help people discover underlying needs that one side may have in common with the other side?

14. *Let people be upset.* Is it permissible to allow someone to be angry, or even loud, when working things out with the other person?

15. *Help people change the system.* The more people we help, the more we may see patterns in the types of conflicts that come up at work. Some of these problems may be caused by prevailing attitudes held by different departments or levels in the company. Others may be caused by—or made worse because of—poorly designed systems or poor communication. Whatever the reasons, should the helper take these problems one step further and help people change the company for a more permanent fix?

16. *Let people not fix it.* Sometimes people decide that they do not want to deal with a conflict. Is it okay for us to let that happen?

17. *Be sure they talk about real issues.* Sometimes people will be fighting about something that they do not want to talk about, so they pick some other issue. One example would be someone becoming upset about a ballpoint pen being borrowed from a desk drawer when the real issue is anger over a lack of privacy. Another example is two middle managers from different departments who cannot agree on what a presentation should look like when what they are really upset about is what one of their bosses said to the other's boss about budget cuts. Should we help people uncover deeper issues?

18. *Stick up for the underdog.* If we think that one person or side is at a disadvantage because of a lack of ability or because of having less power, should we stop helping both sides and work for the underdog?

19. *Make experts.* As we help, should we teach people ways of working on conflict so they can do it without us the next time, or should we only solve the problem and move on?

20. *Stop lawsuits.* Some people feel that if we keep people out of court by helping them with their conflicts, then we may be keeping them from exercising their rights. Should a helper work to keep people from suing one another or the company?

21. *Settle once and for all.* If people make an agreement that works for them now, but does not solve the deeper problem, should the helper reopen the conversation and try to get them to work on the deeper problem or leave it alone?

22. *Convert.* We all are thinking about the best way to handle conflict. As we become more confident of our approach, should we convince people that our way is best?

Debriefing

When you have finished marking the number of votes for each item, summarize what you see on the flip chart. For example: "It looks like we feel strongly that people should be able to get upset and that we need to balance power; we're split when it comes to sticking up for the underdog and converting people to our approach, and almost all of us think that we should stay away from talking about people's beliefs."

Tell the group that each person will have his or her own opinion on how deep is too deep. Remind participants that this workshop is about exposing them to different approaches so that they can develop their own conclusions.

MY PERSONAL CONFLICT STRATEGY

Commentary: Remind participants that the workshop is designed to help them clarify their thinking and to make personal decisions about conflict. Whether we are dealing with a conflict of our own or helping other people with their conflicts, all of us can make choices as we go along. Even when we are in the thick of it, we can step back and make decisions about what we are going to say and do. We are able to make ongoing choices about what we are thinking, what we are saying, and how we are acting. As we go along, we adjust thoughts, words, and actions according to our own theories about conflict or according to what is working at that specific moment.

Choosing Thoughts

Commentary: Tell the group that our thoughts sometimes seem more like reflexes. Often, our mental responses to the other person in a conflict seem automatic and beyond our control—and drive what we say and do.

 Discussion Ask participants: "Can anyone think of an example of when you or someone else reacted automatically in a conflict?"

 Story and Discussion: *The Leaf Blower*
Read (or have someone read) Story 3.1: *The Leaf Blower* to the group, and briefly discuss the story's closing question.

THE LEAF BLOWER

John Pritchett lives alone in the house his parents bought when he was eight years old. John is now eighty-three. He does not go out as often as he used to, but he still enjoys sitting on the porch on a summer evening and watching the neighborhood kids play ball or tag in the street in front of his house. His next-door neighbors, the Junos, moved in about a year and a half ago.

Fred and Patricia Juno bought their house using cash from a wedding present as a large part of their down payment. The house was a fixer-upper when they got it, and they have done most of their own work to get the house the way they want it. Fred spends a great deal of time on his yard. The small front lawn is a manicured carpet of deep green. A white wrought-iron bench encircles an old chestnut tree that shelters the front porch.

John used to chat with the Junos from his front porch, and even lent them tools when they first started their restoration project. He started complaining, however, when they bought a gas-powered leaf blower.

"Makes a lot of noise and more mess than it cleans up," said John. "The same amount of time with a broom and some common courtesy is all you need."

In the autumn, the Junos's chestnut tree drops leaves on the ground, as do many of the other old trees that line the street. John Pritchett has been complaining lately that the Junos's leaves are in his yard and on his driveway. John has even called the police twice telling them that Fred and Patricia are littering in his yard. He says that they intentionally blow the leaves from their yard into his with the leaf blower. The police came out both times but told John there was nothing they could do.

John put a letter in the Junos's mailbox. He called them names in the letter and said that the neighborhood was a good neighborhood before they came in and that they had better watch their step or they would be sorry.

Last Saturday, Patricia took a plate of cookies over to John as a peace offering. John cursed at her through his closed screen door and told her if she didn't get off the porch he would shoot her. Patricia went home and told Fred.

Fred had had about enough of this. He took his cordless telephone out of the house and onto John's front lawn. He waved the telephone at the window and shouted, "I'm calling the cops, you crazy SOB!"

At that moment, John's son Mike drove up with his family. Mike told Fred to get off his father's property. John shouted from the house that he had a gun and was willing to use it.

"So do I, old man," yelled Fred and pulled a small revolver from his waistband. Mike ran back to his car and reached into the glove box for his cell phone. Fred thought Mike was reaching for a gun.

Debriefing
Ask the group:

> *What do you think happened next?*

> *Why do you think that would be how this story would end?*

Commentary: Explain that sometimes our brains work so quickly that it seems as if we have no control over them. People appear to have inevitable responses to situations. "He hit me, so I hit him back."

At other times, it may seem as if we did not think at all.

We can be most helpful to other people—whether we are in conflict with them or helping them with some conflict of their own—if we learn to slow down our thinking. In the book *Getting Past No* (Bantam Books, 1993), William Ury talks about "going to the balcony," a concept he borrowed from fellow Harvard University professor Ronald Heifetz. The idea is that you can picture your conflict occurring on a stage. From time to time it is helpful to "go to the balcony" to monitor your performance.

Tell participants that one way to check their seemingly automatic responses is to take a breath, mentally go to the balcony, and examine their other options.

Stage actors sometimes talk about sitting in the third row during a performance. This is a step beyond calling a mental time-out to go to the balcony. When sitting in the third row, you are watching the entire performance and making adjustments as you go along. Rather than being carried along by the usual exchange of words and actions, you can see what is working moment to moment and make conscious choices. This can keep you from being pulled into inevitable responses like the people in the leaf blower story.

🧍🧍🧍 Group Activity: *A-1, B-2*

For a fun practice, and to illustrate the ability of the brain to adjust quickly from idea to idea, facilitate exercise *A-1, B-2.*

Type
Energizer

Purpose
Wake people up and illustrate the capacity of the brain to switch smoothly among several tasks.

Equipment Needed
None

Preparation
None

Time
5 minutes

Commentary: When we are multitasking, we are actually rapidly switching from one task to another. Sometimes this is a necessary choice to make. When we are listening, our brain will sometimes interject distracting thoughts. For example, in the middle of a meeting, our brain may tell us to remember to pick up bread on the way home. As long as we switch back to the subject at hand, this is not a problem.

When we are sitting in the third row, we want our brains to repeatedly switch focus. We need to focus on what the other person is saying, what we are saying and its impact, the success of the interchange, and our emotional state—all at the same time.

A useful exercise for helping our brains to rapidly switch from one thing to another—a process called multitracking—is called *A-1, B-2*. This exercise was created many years ago by Alice Gachet, an instructor at the Royal Academy of Dramatic Arts in London. Her many talented students included Sir Laurence Olivier, so you will be in good company.

Instructions

Ask participants to stand. Tell them that all they need to know to do this exercise are the English alphabet and how to count to twenty-six in English.

Tell participants that they will be counting and reciting the alphabet at the same time. Demonstrate by reciting, "A-1, B-2, C-3, D-4, E-5, . . ." Then have them do it slowly, as a group. Recite it with them, or help them if they get stuck. After they have arrived at "Z-26" once or twice, ask for volunteers to demonstrate on their own.

If you or someone in the group is especially quick at picking up *A-1, B-2,* you can make the exercise more challenging. Demonstrate (or have a participant who is a quick study demonstrate) by adding a third element or changing the order.

Advanced variations include:

- Adding another memorized element. This can be anything that someone knows by rote. Words to a children's song work well. For example, you can combine "A-1, B-2, . . ." with "Mary Had a Little Lamb": "A-1-Mary, B-2-had, C-3-a, D-4-little, E-5-lamb, F-6-It's, G-7-fleece, H-8-was, . . ."
- Running the exercise backward: "Z-26, Y-25, X-24, W-23, . . ."
- Running the alphabet from both ends: "A-Z, B-Y, C-X, D-W, E-V, . . ."

Debriefing

The more often that you practice *A-1, B-2* on your own, the more effective this exercise will be. Practice while driving, when you are waiting for your computer to boot, or during other idle times. This is a great exercise for warming up your brain before teaching or facilitating. It stimulates while it relaxes and can be helpful before entering a stressful situation. Encourage your group to practice this exercise as a mental warm-up and relaxation technique. Ask people who have children in elementary school to let their kids try it. Children often pick up the exercise very quickly.

Explain that *A-1, B-2* can help us to slow down our thinking so that our minds do not send us speeding down automatic paths.

Commentary: Another way to slow down our thinking is to be sure that we are listening well. Sometimes we tend to listen faster than the other person is thinking. When we do this, we end up responding to what we think the other person is going to say.

"The other person said '*A*,' so I automatically said '*B*,'" is the pattern that emerges. How often do people say, "I was angry," to explain why they said something they later regretted?

Discussion Ask participants to name things that they do to help them pay attention while listening.

Write their ideas on a flip chart and post it. A thorough list of listening techniques will usually include some version of the following items:

- Paraphrase what you have heard to check for clarity.
- Focus on the content of what is being said, not on the speaker or the speaker's manner.
- Take notes.
- Focus on what is most interesting or important to you.
- Listen or watch for emotions that are expressed beyond the words being used.
- Be open to new ideas—listen for things you haven't thought of before.

Once you have completed the list, add whatever you think will be helpful from your own list. Recap the list, and ask for clarification from group members if necessary.

Group Activity: *Listening Practice*

Type
Skill Practice and Feedback

Purpose
Many conflicts at work have to do with what is said and what is understood about what is said. This exercise will help participants to listen not only for words but also for meaning, context, and emotion.

Equipment Needed
- Handout 3.20: Listening Practice Observation Sheet
- Handout 3.21: Listening

Preparation
Make copies of Handout 3.20: Listening Practice Observation Sheet and Handout 3.21: Listening.

Time
25 minutes

Instructions
Separate participants into groups of three each.

Each person will get a turn to tell a brief story of a time when he or she was frustrated by a conflict. When the story is over, another member of the person's group will retell the story using the original storyteller's words, inflections, and emotions as closely as possible. After he or she is finished, the original storyteller will give the person who retold the story feedback about how well the story was retold. Finally, the third partner will give feedback to both of them about the quality of their listening and feedback skills.

Here is an easy way to explain this exercise. You can use a real group from your workshop.

"Rahim, Hope, and Susan are in a group together. Rahim will go first. He will choose someone to listen to his story. Let's say he picks Susan. Rahim will then tell his story to Susan. When the story is done, Susan will then tell the story back to Rahim as Rahim, by using Rahim's words and actions and reflecting Rahim's emotions as much as possible. When Susan is finished, Rahim will tell her how he felt about her retelling. Finally, Hope will offer her feedback about what Susan did and about Rahim's response to it. It may be helpful for Hope to use the observation sheet.

"When Susan is finished with her feedback, another group member will have a turn and so on, until all three have had a chance to tell their stories, have them retold, and receive feedback."

It is sometimes helpful to ask a volunteer to help you demonstrate telling a brief story, having it retold to you, and commenting on it.

Debriefing
When people are finished with the exercise, lead a discussion among all of the groups. If they need prompting, ask them the following questions:

- What did you find out about listening?
- What worked?
- What did not?

Acknowledge that there is more to listening than hearing words alone. Tell the participants that if any of them are interested in more ways to practice better listening, they can read Handout 3.21: Listening at a later time.

LISTENING PRACTICE OBSERVATION SHEET

While the first person tells a story, listen carefully and jot down some key phrases in the box on the left. When the story is repeated, make note of how well the content and emotion are retold.

Key Phrases:

1st Telling	Retelling

Content:
Notes:

Accurate?
[ ] [ ]
yes   no

Emotion:
Notes:

Accurate?
[ ] [ ]
yes   no

Body Language:

Accurate?
[ ] [ ]
yes   no

LISTENING

Listening is the most important skill that we can develop to improve our ability to make conflict productive. We need to ensure that we are focused on what the other person is saying so that we can make good decisions about how we will respond. We need to be certain that communication—the words and actions being presented—flows in every possible direction, and that we are receptive and responsive to everything that is going on.

LISTEN FOR CONTENT

One of the things we need to listen for is content. What is it that the other person is saying? Are you good at listening and remembering what you just heard? Can you listen to a half hour of evening news and then tell someone what was covered, or do you zone out on the couch and catch only odd bits of information?

Try these exercises: Watch the evening news and take notes. Then recap the day's top stories during the last commercial break and see whether your version matches the announcer's recap. You can also do this with a partner. You each take notes and compare them when the program is over. What did you think was important enough to write down? Is that different from what your partner recorded? Do this exercise for a week or so, and see whether you can remember more while taking fewer and fewer notes. Learn your own style for listening and remembering.

One way to determine whether you understand what people are telling you is to repeat it back to them. Ask them whether you got it right: "So you think that we should look at the way we listen to each other, right?" Give them a chance to respond, and listen to the response. They will let you know whether you have it right or not.

LISTEN FOR CONTEXT

Another thing we need to listen for is context. This is everything other than content. It is the big box that content comes to us in. Context may include emotion, the culture of the speaker, the culture of the company, or the speaker's rank in the company relative to yours or to others in the room.

We listen for context not only with our ears but with our eyes and our intuition as well. We also listen for context through a filter of our own beliefs and biases.

If we know what our beliefs and biases are, we can acknowledge them and temporarily put them aside while we listen. (See Handout 3.2: Looking Neutral.)

TIPS FOR FOCUSED LISTENING

It can be difficult to focus while we are listening. Your ears are working, but so is everything else. It is as if there is some kind of traffic jam in your brain. One solution is to fight to keep your mind clear of distractions. Some people will focus on the speaker's lips and words, mentally repeating what is said to keep themselves on track. Although this works well sometimes, a better method may be not to fight our brain's tendency to split its attention.

Either we can acknowledge that there is a lot going on in our brain and make room for one more thing, or we can move the other stuff aside to create a prime spot for what is happening at the moment that we need to be listening to.

Our bodies are like huge clusters of antennae that constantly collect information and send it to our brains. This is good news for us as we send and receive complex messages. The problem is that the signals we want to focus on compete with everything else going on, and with everything else that has ever gone on, and is stored up there in our heads. The brain can be a very noisy place.

You can't fight it, so learn to live with it. You can practice the *A-1, B-2* exercise to help you allow the other information to continue to flow while focusing on what is important at the moment. You will also build your skill to focus while your brain is processing a myriad of information, and you will become better at making decisions about how to respond to what you are experiencing.

Choosing Words

We have all had the experience of making things worse by saying something without thinking. Tell participants that we can also slow our thinking down during a conflict to make better choices about what will come out of our mouths. Another good technique is to spend some time when we aren't in the heat of an argument to look at the way we often say things. The next exercise will help participants find words to use that are less likely to upset the other person in a conflict.

Nontoxic Language

 **Group Activity: *Nontoxic Language***

Type
Brainstorm

Purpose
This is a good companion piece to the listening exercise. Here you can help people think about how their choices of words can color the way that their messages are received.

Equipment Needed
- Flip-chart paper
- Flip Chart 3.3: Nontoxic Language
- Handout 3.22: Reflection Worksheet: Choosing Actions
- Paper
- Pens or pencils

Preparation
Make a copy of Handout 3.22: Reflection Worksheet: Choosing Actions.

Time
15 minutes

Instructions
Ask the workshop participants to take out a piece of paper and make a list of as many printable words or phrases that push their buttons in a conflict as they can think of.

When everyone is finished writing, go around the room and ask each person to give you one phrase from his or her list. Write them on the left-hand side of a flip chart, leaving room for a right-hand column. Keep going around the room until everyone's list is exhausted. Tell participants to cross phrases off their lists if someone else says them first. You should also encourage participants to add any new phrases they think of as you compile the list. Once participants run out of phrases, they should say pass. Your list may look like the left-hand column of Flip Chart 3.3: Nontoxic Language.

If participants are stuck, write some phrases from this list to get them started:

You are lazy.

I hate you.

That was stupid.

You're a liar.

You have a big mouth.

 Trainer Tip: Be aware that some group members may use ethnic slurs on their lists. Decide in advance if you will write these on the flip chart. If someone offers a word that you find inappropriate or extremely offensive, or if it is a word that you do not want to repeat or write down, you can say, "I don't want to put that one on the flip chart. I think I can show you what I mean by using these other words. If—after the exercise—you still think it should be included, let's talk about it on a break."

Write your master list on the left side of the flip chart, leaving the other side blank for additional writing later. If you fill up a flip-chart sheet, tear it off the pad and post it somewhere in the room.

Detoxify

Once you have posted your master list, ask the group to detoxify it. Participants must find a carefully chosen word or phrase that can be used in place of each word on the list. Write it next to the original "toxic" word. Your flip chart may now resemble Flip Chart 3.3: Nontoxic Language.

 Trainer Tip: Some groups will use this as an opportunity to dodge an uncomfortable subject by making jokes (for example, substituting "dirty" with "hygienically challenged"). Tell them you will only accept and write nontoxic words that the group feels will work in real-life situations.

Mention that nontoxic language is not limited to being politically correct or diplomatic. When we choose nontoxic words, we direct our thinking away from belonging to one side or another. It becomes more important for us to communicate clearly than it is to score points against the opposition.

Nontoxic Language

You are lazy.	Help me understand how you choose what is important enough to do.
I hate you.	This makes me angry.
That was stupid.	I don't understand that.
You're a liar.	Our facts don't agree.
You have a big mouth.	

Like leaving our seat to look at the colored ball from all sides, choosing nontoxic language moves us to a new place where new points of view can be considered.

Choosing Actions

 Discussion Ask participants whether anyone can explain the phrase "fight or flight."

Commentary: Fight or flight are the two automatic choices people have when confronting danger, conflict, or other stress. *Fight* means that the stress is met head on. *Flight* means that the stress is avoided.

Tell the group that in this section you will talk about a third choice beyond fight or flight.

 Facilitator: Refer participants to Handout 3.22: Reflection Worksheet: Choosing Actions.

Instructions

Ask the group to fill out Handout 3.22: Reflection Worksheet: Choosing Actions. When they have finished, ask them to talk about their answers for five to ten minutes.

Go around the room and ask participants to name body signals that tell us that we are about to stop thinking clearly. List their responses on a flip chart and post it for future reference.

Some responses you might expect are:

- Tight shoulder or neck muscles
- Faster heart rate
- Shallow breathing
- Flushing or blushing
- Clenched teeth
- Clenched fists

Commentary: Tell the group we all often wish that we could do a conflict situation over again, knowing that if we had made different choices we may have had a different result. Sometimes we wish we had said or done something that we think of later. Sometimes we regret what we did say or do.

REFLECTION WORKSHEET: CHOOSING ACTIONS

We have been talking about "fight or flight." No matter which choice you make, there are advance signals your body sends out that you can use to know that you are about to become aggressive or back down.

Think about these three questions and jot down some thoughts to talk about.

What are some things you feel in your body when you are frightened?

What are some things you feel in your body when you are about to lose your temper?

Do you have ways of calming your body so that you can think more clearly when you are in a conflict situation? What are some of them?

Discussion Ask participants: "Can anyone think of a time when they wished they could have relived a conflict situation?" Participants do not need to speak aloud, but ask them to think of a time when they made poor choices.

Ask them to think of the body signals that may have told them that they were about to stop thinking clearly.

Tell the group that there are many techniques for helping us to relax and think clearly in stressful situations. If members of the group bring up relaxation exercises of their own, then build off of their comments for these exercises or ask them to briefly demonstrate the techniques they used.

Individual Exercise: *Simple Relaxation*

Type
Guided visualization

Purpose
As people become tense, their bodies react in specific ways—such as tight muscles or shallow breathing. A relaxation exercise is an opportunity to reverse the process. Besides being relaxing, this exercise helps people to learn the signals of tenseness in reverse. That is, as they relax, participants will "undo" stress signals. Noting these signals as they go away helps people to recognize them as they appear in stressful situations. This gives them a tool for thinking beyond automatic fight or flight responses to conflict.

Equipment Needed
None

Preparation
None

Time
10 to 15 minutes

 Facilitator: In this exercise, you will guide the group through a simple relaxation exercise. Because this may be foreign to some people, the exercise is written to make it as nonthreatening as possible. You can read this script word for word, learn it and use your own words, use a similar exercise of your own, or use a recorded relaxation exercise. The main point of the exercise is for people to recognize what their bodies do while they are relaxed. Learning this helps people to recognize the signals that the body sends when under stress. Recognizing the relaxed and stressed signals helps people to know when they need to take a break or change their pace to remain calm in a conflict situation.

Instructions

Begin by explaining the entire exercise. When you speak, use a calm, soothing tone, and breathe evenly along with the group.

Commentary: We have talked about how our bodies signal us when we are beginning to feel stress. We can direct some of these same signals—clenching of the jaw, tightening of the face and throat, or shallow breathing—in the other direction so that our minds become calm. When you notice, for example, that your throat is tightening, you can "tell" it to relax. This becomes easier to do if you teach your body how to relax when you are not under stress.

There is a saying, "We do not sing because we are happy; we are happy because we sing." The idea is that we can send physical signals from our body to tell our mind how to feel.

Tell participants, "I am going to talk you through an exercise that you can use on your own to learn to relax. When we do this exercise, you will close your eyes. I will ask you to take three deep breaths to get started. Then you will start at the top of your head and I will ask you to relax muscle by muscle to the tips of your toes.

"We will then breathe some more, and I will ask you to continue to relax by counting backward from ten to one. This is not hypnotism. You will be in control at all times. I am merely showing you an exercise you can use by yourself to train your body to respond to your desire to relax.

"After the countdown, I will count to three and you will use your imagination to picture yourself in a beautiful place in nature. Maybe a favorite place or a place you have always wanted to go. Somewhere with sun and shade, maybe some running water. You will imagine every detail—the temperature of the air, the light, the colors, the smells, everything.

"We'll spend a little time relaxing there, and then we'll slowly come back to the workshop. You'll find yourself relaxed and refreshed.

"Ready?"

 Facilitator: Now lead the visualization.

Speak slowly while saying to participants, "Please sit comfortably in your chairs. . . . Loosen any neckties or collars or anything that will keep you from breathing comfortably. . . . Take a slow, deep breath with me. . . . In. . . . Out. . . . Another one. . . . In. . . . Out. . . . One more. . . . Good. . . .

"Feel yourself relax into the chair. . . . Relax the muscles in your face, especially the little muscles around the corners of your eyes. . . . When these relax, the rest will follow. . . .

"Relax your scalp and your forehead. . . . Breathe deeply. . . .

"Relax your face. . . . Your eyes. . . . Your lips. . . .

"Relax your tongue. . . . Let it just lie there. . . . Breathe. . . .

"Relax your neck and your throat. . . . Breathe. . . .

"Take a deep breath and let it out slowly as your shoulders and arms relax. . . .

"Let your hands sit on the arms of the chair, the table, your lap—wherever you have them. . . . Let them just sit. . . . Relax your hands and wrists and fingers. . . .

"Relax your stomach. . . . Breathe. . . .

"Imagine the slow deep breaths you are taking are traveling down your legs to the soles of your feet. . . . Breathe in. . . . Down your legs to the soles of your feet. . . . Breathe out. . . .

"Breathe. . . .

"Now we are going to count down from ten to one.

"Breathe and relax the little muscles at the corner of your eyes. . . . Listen while I count. . . ."

 Facilitator: Speak slowly, allow for a deep breath between each number, and breathe along with the group.

---

ten [breathe]

nine [breathe]

eight [breathe]

seven [breathe]

six [breathe]

five [breathe]

four [breathe]

three [breathe]

two [breathe]

one [breathe]

"Now picture yourself in a beautiful place in nature. Breathe. . . . Where is it? . . . Where are you sitting? . . . Feel the sun or the shade. . . . Breathe. . . . Are there birds? . . . Is there wind? . . . Can you hear rushing water? . . .

"Breathe. . . . Relax. . . . I'm going to be quiet for a while so that you can enjoy where you are. . . . The more detail you put in, the more relaxed you will be. . . . Any outside noise will just become a part of your beautiful place in nature. . . ."

 Facilitator: Wait at least two or three minutes. When it feels like the group is ready, continue.

"I am going to count back to ten. . . . One . . . two . . . three . . . four . . . five . . . six . . . seven . . . eight . . . nine . . . ten.

"Open your eyes. Look around. Welcome back."

Debriefing

People usually "come to" with big smiles. Give them a chance to rub their eyes, laugh, and talk with the people around them.

Ask the group how it felt.

Reiterate that what they did was tell their bodies what to do to relax. They gave their bodies the opposite commands that they get from fight or flight. Remind them that this did not take long, and encourage them to practice relaxation when they have free time—at their desks or before falling asleep at night.

Ask participants whether they think that this type of simple relaxation exercise might help them stay calm in conflict situations.

Commentary: If the group enjoyed the *Simple Relaxation* exercise and you have additional time, tell participants that a quick way to relax is to notice your own breath. Explain that if you are accustomed to practicing relaxation, you can focus on your breath going in and out. It helps to clear the mind. Ask participants to close their eyes again and relax. Tell them to say "breathe in" when the air is coming into their bodies, and "breathe out" when they exhale. This technique can be useful when you feel yourself losing control of your responses to other people.

 Facilitator: Refer participants to Handout 3.23: Tips for Calm Listening for other ways to use relaxation to help them listen better.

Summarize the section by saying that there are many ways to overcome the tendency to react without thinking: going to the balcony; sitting in the third row; listening well; and controlling the symptoms of stress in our bodies so that we can choose our thoughts, words, and actions.

OUR GROUP CONFLICT STRATEGY

 Facilitator: This section of the workshop answers the question "Now what?" for practical people and "So what?" for skeptical ones.

 Group Activity: *Action Plan*

Type
Action Plan

Purpose
Help participants bring together the diverse experiences of the workshop. Help participants carry what they have learned back to the workplace.

TIPS FOR CALM LISTENING

We sometimes try to focus on listening by talking to our brain as if it were a pesky pet: "Not now, brain. I'm listening!" The harder we push against our brain's tendency to switch from one topic to another, the harder it seems to push back: "But you mustn't forget to pick up your dry cleaning tomorrow!"

A way to calm your brain is to make a promise to it. Keep a pad of paper near you while you are listening, and write notes to yourself as stray thoughts pop into your head. This will keep your brain happy and it won't bring up the topic again for a while. It's true you won't be listening 100 percent while you jot down "dry cleaning, Tues., PM," but you will be distracted for a shorter period of time by this than by trying to seesaw between telling your brain to pipe down and focusing on what you want to be listening to. The trick here is to not only take notes on what is being said to you, but to separately jot down your distractions. Promise your brain you'll get back to it later.

One approach for managing the traffic in your brain is to turn down the volume on everything except what is happening at the moment. This is difficult or even impossible to do if you try to force your brain to behave. Instead, think of your brain as a flowing river full of fascinating objects. Pick up the objects you are interested in at the moment, and let the other ones flow by. They will be back when you need them.

Try closing your eyes and sitting quietly before a meeting or conversation that you think will require calm listening. Have you ever noticed your own breath? Try not to make yourself breathe at any particular rate; merely observe your breathing. When you breathe in, say, "Breathe in" to yourself; when you breathe out, say, "Breathe out." It takes a little practice; but focusing on your breath will seem to clear your mind of everything else. Notice three breaths in a row and open your eyes. The next thing you see or hear will take a prime position in your mind.

If you notice yourself being distracted while someone is speaking, try noticing three breaths. Feel yourself breathe and think, "Breathe in, breathe out," with each cycle. You won't be listening to the other person for the ten seconds this takes, but when you tune back in, you will be absolutely focused. (You weren't listening anyway, and this simple exercise will clear your mind more quickly than trying to say, "Down, boy!" to your brain or emotions.)

Here is a list of simple tools that will help you to stay focused while listening. Pick the one that you are most comfortable with, or use them all in combination.

Tools for Staying Focused While Listening

1. Take notes of what the speaker is saying—and check to see whether you are getting it right.

2. Train yourself to multitrack—"A-1, B-2, C-3, . . . " It will help you to become accustomed to sorting through all the signals to focus on the one you want.

3. Take notes on what is distracting you—and promise your brain that you will get back to it.

4. Calm your mind. If you're not listening well anyway, take a ten-second break and notice three breaths. You'll listen better when you "come back."

Equipment Needed

- Flip-chart paper
- Markers
- Flip Chart 3.4: How Should We Do This?
- Handout 3.24: Action Plan

Preparation

Make five copies of Flip Chart 3.4: How Should We Do This? and sufficient copies of Handout 3.24: Action Plan for each participant.

Time

40 to 60 minutes

Instructions

1. *Handout:* Ask the group to fill in Handout 3.24: Action Plan.

2. *Group Consensus:* When they have finished, break them into small groups. Give participants five minutes to see whether each group can come to some consensus on three points that answer the question "What should we do?" Be sure that the groups focus only on this question. The question, "Why should we do it?" is there to help them think and to help with reasons for the "What should we do?" question, if necessary.

   Remind the groups that they have learned and practiced consensus-building techniques that may help them if they get stuck.

3. *Large Group Discussion:* At the end of five minutes, ask for a report from each group. See whether you can find common ground among each subgroup's "What should we do?" answers. Try to obtain agreement from all the groups on three to five actions. Be sure that everyone is heard, and use the yes-no-pass method if the group gets stuck.

4. *Yes, No, or Pass:* If necessary, go around the room again, this time asking each person to vote out loud yes, no, or pass for the number one "What should we do" answer. If everyone votes yes on an answer, that will be included in the action plan.

   Here is what to do when you get no or pass votes. Once everyone has voted on a specific answer, ask for comments from anyone who voted no or pass.

   Allow the no or pass voters to persuade others or to be persuaded. When the discussion on a particular answer is complete, go around the room again and ask for yes, no, or pass votes. Have more discussion, and then vote again. If two rounds do not get consensus, move on to the next answer. If you get an answer that everyone votes yes on, that will be included in the action plan.

   If intonation or body language indicates to you that someone is not happy with his or her vote (for example, if you think that someone is going along because he or she feels pressured), draw the person out.

How Should We Do This?

Action:

Who:

When:

Completion
Criteria:

ACTION PLAN

1. What Should We Do?

Consider everything you know about conflict and write three reasonable things your workshop group can do to make conflict a positive experience for the company.

A.

B.

C.

2. Why Is That So Important

Make a one- or two-sentence business case and/or a one- or two-sentence personal case for each of the three things you have listed.

A.

B.

C.

Commentary: Over the last two days we have been collecting experiences, testing ideas, and learning about conflict and each other.

The action plan is an important part of the workshop. This is where all of the exercises, reflection, discussion, and thinking comes together. Action planning can be the difference between a workshop being merely a couple of nice days or having some lasting effect.

 Facilitator: Be sure that you are using the group's word for conflict *as much as possible.*

Action Planning

When you have your list of three to five actions, ask the large group to brainstorm the next step of the action plan. To do this, take each action one at a time, and write the group's answers to the following questions on Flip Chart 3.4: How Should We Do This?:

1. Who should do this?
2. How will we know we have done or are doing this?
3. When should this be done, or when is our first progress point?

When you have a list of everyone's best answers, work for consensus on the list. First, see if there are answers that are very close and ask the group for permission to eliminate duplicate answers or to combine answers to make a new answer. Do not get bogged down in writing beautifully constructed statements. If the group is concerned about the wording, a subgroup can wordsmith your action plan later. If the group gets stuck, use the yes-no-pass method to break the logjam.

If at any time a minority opinion cannot be changed, include it on a separate minority report list. If you have time, you can come back to this list to see whether the majority and minority differences can be reconciled.

When you have a list that everyone can agree on for your action plan, read it over and ask the group whether it makes sense. If you have time, it is a good idea to have a brief discussion about any obstacles to implementing the action plan successfully that the group may have.

CLOSE

Commentary: Ask participants to refer back to the objectives they had for the workshop. If there are any unchecked items from the group's individual objectives, check to see how close you came to meeting them.

Trainer Tip: In some organizations, you may want an alternative to a group action plan. One idea is to ask individuals to list and discuss five things they will do differently as a result of the workshop. Listing one or two things is easy, but asking for five helps people to think more deeply. Even if you aren't able to write an action plan with a structured follow-up process, discussing these lists makes them public and can generate new ideas for going forward.

Tell the participants that they have made a major contribution to the workshop, and that you would like it to continually evolve.

Evaluation

Ask participants to fill in the evaluation form in Handout 3.25: Level One Evaluation.

Finally, thank participants for their hard work and remind them of what they have accomplished.

Trainer Tip: A lively ending to the workshop is to repeat the *Bell Curve* exercise from the beginning and ask people to comment. If you have a quieter group, you can skip repeating the exercise and merely remind them of it. Ask them to think about where they stood on each question, and have them picture where they would stand now that they have completed the workshop.

LEVEL ONE EVALUATION

Today's Date: _____

Thank you for the opportunity to serve you with this program. Your opinions and ideas are extremely valuable. Through your feedback, we can continually improve this and other training courses. Please be honest and constructive. Thank you—we value your thoughts and suggestions.

Please circle the number that most accurately represents your thoughts. Please comment on any item.

1   Unsatisfactory—Did Not Meet My Expectations
2   Fair—Met Some of My Expectations
3   Good—Met My Expectations
4   Very Good—Exceeded Some of My Expectations
5   Excellent—Exceeded All of My Expectations

    1. Logistics of training session:

       a. Meeting room facilities   1 2 3 4 5

       b. Dates and times   1 2 3 4 5

    Comments:

    2. Overall information presented   1 2 3 4 5

    Comments:

3. Facilitator's knowledge and expertise   1   2   3   4   5

Comments:

4. Facilitator's interaction with group   1   2   3   4   5

Comments:

Please rate the discussion and activities of the following topic sections in terms of how useful you found them to be in helping to improve or enhance your conflict skills.

1   Not Useful
2   Less Useful
3   Useful
4   More Useful
5   Very Useful

5. Naming the Workshop   1   2   3   4   5

Comments:

6. Ways of Seeing   1   2   3   4   5

Comments:

7. Stories about taking a second look   1   2   3   4   5

Comments:

8. Ways of Seeing Conflict (Win, Lose, or Draw/Even,   1 2 3 4 5
   Bigger, Different)

   Comments:

9. Two Sisters and One Orange   1 2 3 4 5

   Comments:

10. Reflection Sheets   1 2 3 4 5

    Comments:

11. Party Time Discussion and Debates   1 2 3 4 5

    Comments:

12. Mediation Practice   1 2 3 4 5

    Comments:

13. My Personal Conflict Strategy   1 2 3 4 5

    Comments:

14. Action Planning/Group Conflict Strategy   1   2   3   4   5

    Comments:

15. What topic/discussion was of the most value to you?
    Please explain:

16. What topic/discussion was of the least value to you?
    Please explain:

17. **General Comments:**

Thanks!

PART THREE

PARTICIPANT WORKBOOK

Handouts

PREWORKSHOP MEMO

Date:

To:

From:

Re: *Conflict Management Skills Workshop*

Welcome to the *Conflict Management Skills Workshop*. This exciting two-day session will give us the opportunity to examine our current approaches to conflict, and decide how to change them if we need to.

We will be looking at where our ideas about conflict come from, how we feel about conflict at work, and how we think we can improve.

As a group, we will decide what we can do to make conflict at work a constructive force here at our company.

Please take a few minutes to fill out this questionnaire and return it anonymously to _____ no later than _____. Your responses will help us to prepare a workshop that best serves the needs of the group.

I look forward to seeing you on _____ at _____. We have a great deal of work to do, so please be prompt.

Thank you for your assistance.

PREWORKSHOP QUESTIONNAIRE

Please answer this quick questionnaire and return it to _____ by _____. Your answers will help us ensure that the workshop is a practical tool that is specific to your needs.

5 = Strongly Agree; 4 = Agree; 3 = Disagree; 2 = Strongly Disagree; 1 = Don't Know

1. I am good at handling conflict at work. 5 4 3 2 1

2. I would rather avoid conflict than meet it head-on. 5 4 3 2 1

3. I think what is right is worth fighting for. 5 4 3 2 1

4. Some things are not worth fighting about. 5 4 3 2 1

5. Only fight when you know you are going to win. 5 4 3 2 1

6. If I disagree with people at work, I will never get them to do the things that are important to me. 5 4 3 2 1

7. I think we handle differences effectively here at our company. 5 4 3 2 1

8. I am happy with the way that I deal with daily conflict. 5 4 3 2 1

9. What causes conflict among people who work together at our company?

_____

_____

_____

_____

_____

10. I think that our company is

    ❏ More able than   ❏ About the same as   ❏ Less able than

    other companies when it comes to dealing effectively with conflict.

11. I think that I am

    ❏ More able than   ❏ About the same as   ❏ Less able than

    other people when it comes to dealing effectively with conflict.

WORKSHOP OBJECTIVES

INTRODUCTION

Welcome to your *Conflict Management Skills Workshop.* Look around at all of the other people who are in the workshop with you. No two of us have had all of the same experiences. Everyone in the workshop, including you, has come to some conclusion about conflict. Some people think conflict is a good thing. Some think it should be avoided at all costs.

We each have a point of view about conflict that comes from what has or has not worked for us and from our beliefs about how we should live our lives. Everyone in the workshop is a philosopher. All of us have theories about conflict and what to do with it.

OBJECTIVES

- During the two days of this workshop, you will have the opportunity to think about your point of view on conflict.

- You will have the opportunity to compare notes with the other people in the workshop.

- You will be able to test your point of view.

- You will have the opportunity to change your mind and influence others.

- You will have the opportunity to come to some agreement with your coworkers about ways to think about and respond to conflict at work.

- You will have a chance to remember what you already know about conflict, learn from others, and arrange all these ideas into your own practical theory.

- You will have a chance to join problem-solving sessions, speak up with new ideas, and learn about other people's points of view.

- You should be able to make decisions about how you will handle conflict as an individual and as part of this group.

MODULE I OBJECTIVES

INTRODUCTION

It is time to compare notes with other people in the workshop.

There is a saying that fish never talk about the water. What this means is that when we are involved in something every day or see something every day, we stop noticing it. We respond to it as if it is simply the way things are— or the way things must be.

Our relationship with conflict is similar. In this module, we examine the points of view that each one of us has developed about conflict over the years. There may be some surprises. Sometimes what we think about conflict and how we deal with it have become so automatic that we take these methods for granted. Most of us rarely take the time to think about conflict or to evaluate whether what we have figured out about conflict is working as well as we would like.

OBJECTIVES

- As we open the session, you will begin deciding on the direction of the workshop that works best for you.

- We will work together to find the best name for conflict at our company.

- We will learn what other people think about conflict and compare it with our own points of view.

- You will have the opportunity to think about any new ideas that you would like to consider.

GROUP ONE INSTRUCTIONS

Use everything that you know about conflict to work with group two and group three on the situation written on the flip chart.

Group four will not speak during this exercise. They are here only to observe and take notes.

GROUP TWO INSTRUCTIONS

Use everything that you know about conflict to work with group one and group three on the situation written on the flip chart. Group four will not speak during this exercise. They are here only to observe and take notes.

As a member of group two, you belong to a unique cultural group that has a special set of behaviors. During the exercise, you need to follow these behaviors very strictly.

Group Two's Behaviors:

❏ Women can speak to any man or woman.

❏ Men can speak to any man.

❏ Men can only speak to a woman in their own group if spoken to first by that woman.

❏ Men can only respond to women in the other groups through a woman in their own group.

❏ Direct eye contact is considered extremely rude.

❏ Smiling when saying maybe means no.

GROUP THREE INSTRUCTIONS

Use everything that you know about conflict to work with group one and group two on the situation written on the flip chart. Group four will not speak during this exercise. They are here only to observe and take notes.

As a member of group three, you belong to a unique cultural group that has a special set of beliefs. During the exercise, you need to follow these beliefs very strictly.

Group Three's Beliefs:

❏ You believe strongly that any time anyone is in a training exercise that goes more than three minutes beyond its allotted time, it will shorten that person's life span by five years.

❏ You, as a member of group three, care about the welfare of your fellow human beings above everything else.

GROUP FOUR INSTRUCTIONS

Use everything that you know about conflict as you observe groups one, two, and three working together on the situation described on the flip chart. You must not speak or offer any help during this exercise. You are here only to observe and take notes. It may be best if you and your group members split up and watch specific people or groups during the exercise.

You may want to use this checklist to help you take notes.

Things to watch for:

❑ Displays of frustration or impatience

❑ Displays of open hostility or anger

❑ Name calling

❑ Uses of humor (positive or negative)

❑ Asking questions about why people are behaving differently from usual

❑ Attempts to explain why people are behaving differently from usual

❑ What incidents cause what reactions

❑ Any juicy quotes that may illustrate how the exercise is going

❑ Anything else of interest

WAYS OF SEEING CONFLICT

We all have our own attitudes and beliefs about the world around us. Sometimes these points of view come from our experiences. Sometimes we have stayed up nights thinking about them. Sometimes we have learned them from someone we respect. Sometimes our points of view just feel "right."

Some points of view are so much a part of us that we cannot begin to think about where they came from. They are just part of whom we are. Often, we believe that these points of view are worth fighting over. They may be, but sometimes a conflict will go on indefinitely because we start fighting about different points of view instead of what the conflict was about in the first place. Once this happens, we can become stuck in a conflict.

To get unstuck, we need to take a look at the point of view that we are defending and figure out where it came from and whether it still makes sense.

Let us say that I cannot go to sleep because I am convinced that there is a monster under the bed. I can check my point of view if I get up and look under the bed. Before I get into a conflict defending a point of view that I am absolutely certain of, it makes sense for me to look under the bed for myself. This way, I can check my point of view to see whether it is based on good information.

I should also check to see whether the information I have leads directly to the point of view. If I hear a noise in the dark, does it always mean that there is a monster under my bed? The information that there is a noise is good information, but I won't know if my point of view makes sense until I get up and turn on the light.

Sometimes our points of view have been with us for so long that it seems like they just grew up out of nowhere—which can make it difficult to figure out where they came from. The following pages cover material that might help you recognize:

- The way you see the world
- The way you are certain that something is true
- The way you learn about new things
- The way you look at conflict itself

Ways of Seeing

Sometimes, people can get into a conflict because they have different ways of looking at the world. Although some differences among people—such as religion or culture—may be obvious to us, it is good to remember that there are plenty of other ways of seeing things that put people in conflict with each other. We all come from different backgrounds, whether we grew up next door to one another or on opposite sides of the world. We all have different experiences that shape the way we look at things. This means that we all end up with different lists of what is important to us. Sometimes we get into conflict over which list is the correct one.

Ways of Knowing

Sometimes we argue or even go to war about what we know to be true. Can there be more than one so-called truth? People have different ways of deciding what is true. There is religious truth; scientific truth; truth that we reason for ourselves; and truth that we learn from a teacher, parent, or some other respected source. Sometimes, we use a combination of these ways of knowing to figure out what is true.

Here are some questions you can ask yourself when you are disagreeing with someone about what is true:

- Where did I get the information that led me to believe that this is true?
- Could someone with different information come to a different conclusion?
- Could someone with the same information come to a different conclusion?
- If the other person's information and sources of information were mine, would I come to the other person's conclusion?

Ways of Learning

People learn differently from one another. Sometimes this can cause confusion, which leads to conflict.

People learn new things either by trial and error, by watching something happen, by thinking about the information offered to them, or by feeling strongly about what is being learned. People also either accept information based on the authority of whoever is telling it to them or like to argue about or think about it on their own and form their opinions that way.

If one person likes to read information and then sit quietly and think about it before coming to a conclusion, while the other person prefers being part of a discussion about the information and coming to a quick conclusion, they might find something to argue about. They might not argue about the conclusion, but they may have trouble agreeing about the best way to get there.

Along the same line, if one person believes strongly that what we learn from a favorite teacher or book is always true, and the other person believes that the best way to figure out what is true is by having a debate, then they may have a difficult time agreeing.

Ways of Seeing Conflict

It is also important to take a good look at how we feel about conflict. Sometimes people see conflict differently from one another and end up fighting about that. Ask yourself the following questions:

- Do I think that conflict is something bad that I should avoid, or something positive that will help me to learn new things?

- Is conflict always a contest, with a clear winner and loser?

- Is conflict ever an opportunity to create something new?

Sometimes people need to agree about how to look at the disagreement before they can look at the disagreement itself. In this workshop, we explore two ways of seeing conflict: "Win, Lose, or Draw" and "Make It Even, Make It Bigger, or Make It Different."

When you learn the way that you look at conflict, you can figure out how to approach it.

Win, lose, or draw is what we call the point of view that in every conflict there are only three possible outcomes for each party. You win, you lose, or there is some kind of a tie. If you see conflict as a win, lose, or draw situation, your best approach is to plan on how you are going to beat the other person. If you do not figure out how to win, you will end up with the short end of the stick.

If you see conflict as a chance to make it even, make it bigger, or make it different, then you will try to use a conflict situation to improve on whatever has been going on so far.

The make-it-even approach means dividing something even-steven so that both sides split whatever is being fought over right down the middle or dividing it in whatever way will make everybody feel like they got a good deal.

The make-it-bigger approach means that you figure out how to get more of whatever is being fought over. Not enough stuff to go around? Then work together to figure out how to get more stuff and divide it up.

The make-it-different approach means that you decide to work together on something other than whatever the fight was about at first. The fight may appear to be about one thing, for example, getting a fair share of stuff. A different look may show other possible causes. Maybe the whole thing concerns the way someone feels about conflict. It could concern the way someone feels about the way stuff has been divided up in the past or other deeper issues. In the make-it-different scenario, we find something different about the disagreement so that we can see it in a new way. For example, there may not be a way to get more stuff at the moment, but we may find out that both sides feel the same way about the way stuff has been divided up in the past.

When we make it different, we find solutions to the problem or we learn about one another by focusing on a part of the conflict that makes sense to everybody. We may not get more stuff when we look at how we have shared stuff in the past, but we may gain a better understanding of why we are fighting about stuff in the first place.

What Do I Think About Conflict Right Now?

Handout 1.7: Reflection Worksheet: What Do I Think About Conflict Right Now? is the first of a series of four reflection worksheets that you can use to think about what you are getting out of this workshop.

This workshop is designed to help you clarify your own points of view about conflict. The reflection sheets will help you organize everything you have been hearing, reading, and talking about up to that point. There is no need to tell anyone what is on your reflection sheet unless you want to. Reflection sheets are included to give you a chance to take a breath, slow down your brain, and examine old points of view or build new ones.

REFLECTION WORKSHEET: WHAT DO I THINK ABOUT CONFLICT RIGHT NOW?

Are there times when one side winning and another side losing is the only appropriate solution? When?

Can I think of three things that I will always fight for, no matter what?

What do most people fight about here at my company: ways of seeing, ways of knowing, ways of learning, ways of living, or ways of seeing conflict?

What are some other causes of conflict at my company?

MODULE 2 OBJECTIVES

INTRODUCTION

What you think and feel about conflict can determine how you respond to it.

OBJECTIVES

- In this module you will examine what makes you respond the way that you do in conflict situations.
- You will think about whether conflict can be a positive thing for you, for other people, or for the company.
- You will think about whether you should change some of the ways you respond to conflict.

REFLECTION WORKSHEET: "GOOD" CONFLICT?

Can you think of some conflicts that may have seemed uncomfortable or were unpleasant but produced good results?

Can you think of any conflicts that produced more good than they cost?

Can you think of any conflicts that people would be willing to go through again because of the good that came of them?

Can you think of a time here at our company when there was a difference between groups, individuals, or with a client or supplier and something good came out of facing it head on?

How could this have been handled to make it even better?

What makes it difficult to handle conflicts the way you just suggested?

PARTY DESCRIPTIONS

After reading over these brief descriptions, join the party that best matches the way you feel most comfortable when dealing with conflict.

- The Puzzle Party
  People in the Puzzle Party know that each conflict can be figured out if they approach it analytically and are dedicated to finding an answer.

- The Persuasion Party
  Persuasion Party members know that the best way to deal with conflict is to be sure that people see why it is in their best interest to adjust their positions and move on.

- The Palm Tree Party
  Palm trees can weather any storm. Palm Tree Party members know that if they bend enough, the conflict will pass over them. They may be shaken up when it is over, but they will survive.

- The Personal Party
  Personal Party people know that if they respect the other side and acknowledge their ideas and feelings (even if they disagree), the conflict will become secondary to what they learn about one another.

REFLECTION WORKSHEET: HOW CAN THIS POSSIBLY BE GOOD FOR ME?

As you think about and answer the questions on this reflection worksheet, think of a specific conflict situation at work that you have been a part of, will be a part of, should be a part of, or would like to be a part of.

WIIFM? *(What's in it for me?)*
What might I gain by being a part of this conflict?

What might I learn by being a part of this conflict?

What might change about me as a result of being a part of this conflict?

WIIFOP? *(What's in it for the other person?)*
What might the other person(s) gain because I am a part of this conflict?

WIIFU? *(What's in it for us?)*
What might everyone involved gain because I am a part of this conflict?

What might my team or department and I gain because I am a part of this conflict?

What might the company gain because I am a part of this conflict?

Can groups of people (teams, departments, or companies) learn from conflict? If they can, what can they learn?

So?
If there are benefits to conflict, should you wait for conflict to come to the surface by itself, or should you look for hidden conflict and intentionally bring it up?

What would you do if you decide to constructively leave conflict alone? What would you do if you decide to constructively bring conflict to the surface?

MODULE 3 OBJECTIVES

INTRODUCTION

We will now look at various ways of dealing with conflict. This will help us—as individuals and as a group—make decisions about how to handle conflicts here at work.

In this module, we will briefly review approaches to helping other people with their conflicts by acting as a neutral third party. We will also come to conclusions about what form of help is most appropriate at work.

OBJECTIVES

- You will test information about helping other people with their conflicts.
- You will have the opportunity to think about and discuss what types of help are best for you to offer when you are at work.
- You will make decisions about what you and the group should do about conflicts at work.

LOOKING NEUTRAL

Sometimes we are asked to help someone who is in a conflict situation. We may be asked to take sides, or we may be asked to get in the middle as a neutral party to help sort things out.

Can we truly be neutral? To most of us, the word *neutral* means not taking sides. And we may be able to do that. We will still believe what we believe, and this may include an opinion about who is right and who is wrong.

When we decide not to take sides, we are neutral on the outside, but we still have our beliefs and points of view on the inside. That is, we "look" neutral.

Looking neutral might include not voicing an opinion, ensuring that everyone involved in the conflict is heard, and keeping people safe. We might look neutral by carefully choosing words so that they do not support one side or another. Looking neutral might also include keeping confidences—not telling the other side something that someone has told you in confidence.

Looking neutral is not dishonest. You are not going to stop being yourself while you help people with their differences. However, you are going to behave in a way that makes people feel sure that you will be as evenhanded as possible.

One way to be sure that you look neutral to the people you are trying to help is to check with them. When people ask you to help them as a neutral party, tell them what looking neutral looks like to you and see whether that works for them. If everybody can agree to what neutral looks like, you have a better picture of how you can help.

Here are some things to think about as you work on your own definition of what neutral looks like:

- What points of view do I have that might make it hard to look neutral?
  - Do I know something about the people or the situation that will make it hard for me to manage the way I react?
  - Do I know my hot buttons—things that can make me respond emotionally?
  - Do I have preconceived ideas about the people I have been asked to help?
  - Do I have preconceived ideas about the type of situation I have been asked to help with?

- What relationships or positions do I have that might make it hard to look neutral? Even as I work hard to be fair and look neutral, could somebody accuse me of having a conflict of interest?
  - Do I have a close friend or relative involved?
  - Does my job title or position make it difficult for me to look neutral?
  - Does any group I belong to make it hard for me to look neutral?
  - Is there a way to deal with these relationships or positions so that everyone feels I can still be of help?

- Are there any secrets I am not willing to keep?
  - What if someone tells me about a crime?
  - What if someone threatens violence?
  - What if someone breaks company policy?

- Is there a certain person or group that I feel usually needs to be protected from any other person or group?
  - Do I feel like I need to stick up for the underdog?
  - Do I need to defend company policy?

- If people come up with agreements or plans that I think are wrong or harmful, will I speak up?
  - If I think the plan won't work or won't last, should I say so?
  - If I think the plan is not fair to one side or the other, should I speak up?
  - If the plan involves dangerous or criminal activity, should I try to stop it?
  - Does the plan need to operate within company policy?

- Do I need to tell people my answers to these questions before I help them?

There are not necessarily right or wrong answers to any of these questions. The point is that the more you know about yourself and your point of view before deciding to look neutral, the better.

TWO SIBLINGS AND ONE ORANGE— TAKE ONE: PROBLEM-SOLVING MEDIATION SCRIPT

People:

    Mediator—Tony
    Sibling 1—Jerry
    Sibling 2—Sandy

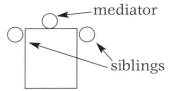

Set up a table with three chairs. The chairs for the two siblings face one another across the table. Tony's chair is between them. As the siblings come in, Tony greets them and asks them to take a seat. When both siblings are seated, Tony takes a seat.

Tony: I understand that there is some problem about an orange between you two?

Jerry: I'll say! This jerk knows that I need the orange, and . . .

Sandy: *(interrupting)* That's exactly like Jerry! Everything is about what *Jerry* needs. . . .

Tony: *(interrupting)* Let's wait just a minute, Sandy. Jerry, you too. I need to tell you how this will work. Most important, you both need to know that I'm not here to make any decisions for you. This isn't like court where you tell me things and I decide for you. This is an opportunity for the two of you to sit down together, talk about what the problem is, and figure out a solution that works for both of you. How does that sound?

Jerry: I have a solution in mind already. We just have to get through to Simple Simon over there.

Tony: Right now I need to know that you are both willing to work together on this problem. You will get a chance to tell your story, Jerry. For now, tell me if you are willing to talk this out.

Jerry: Sure. I'll stay if Sandy stays.

Tony: Sandy?

Sandy: I'll stay, but Jerry has to stop calling me names.

Tony: Good. In fact, why don't we make that a ground rule for our meeting? "No name-calling."

The siblings nod their agreement.

Tony: Here's how this will work. Everything you tell me will be confidential. I won't tell anyone about what we talk about here unless you want me to. You may see me take notes so I can keep my thinking straight, but you'll also see me tear my notes up when we are finished. I won't take sides but will be here to be sure that you both are represented and to help you figure this out.

We'll start by having each of you bring me up to date on what the problem is. First one will speak and then the other. During that time, I don't want you to interrupt—just listen. If there is something you want to be sure to say, write it down and say it during your turn.

Once you have had your turns, we can ask questions and talk about different points of view. If we come up with a solution that works for both of you, we'll write it down and sign it.

Sound good?

Sandy and Jerry nod.

Tony: Who would like to go first?

Sandy: It may as well be Jerry. Jerry always goes first.

Jerry: All right, I will.

Tony: Is that really all right, Sandy?

Sandy: Yeah.

Jerry: Sandy has this self-image of being a great chef or something. I came home from running and wanted some fresh orange juice. It's full of antioxidants and vitamin C. I need it after a run, but—no! Sandy has to bake. I'm hot, I'm tired, I'm thirsty. So all I did was pick up the orange and start to walk out of the room. . . .

Sandy: I was using it!!!

Tony: *(calmly)* You'll get your turn, Sandy.

Jerry: See how Sandy always interrupts and yells? Anyway, I picked up the orange. . . .

Sandy: I do not interrupt and yell!

Tony: *(still calm, but a little more firmly)* Sandy, let's let Jerry finish. You may want to write down what you were going to say so you don't forget it.

(Sandy writes furiously on the tablet on the table: "I don't yell!!!")

Tony: Jerry?

Jerry: I picked up the orange and started to go out of the room and Sandy came after me screaming that the orange wasn't mine, that it was part of some recipe.

(There is a pause.)

Tony: Anything else, Jerry?

Jerry: That's about all there was to it. All I wanted was to make some orange juice.

Tony: Thanks. Now, Sandy, why don't you . . .

Sandy: I was using that orange! Jerry just waltzes in and grabs the orange without asking and I need the entire peel to grate into my special Blue Ribbon Pound Cake. It's just like Jerry to ignore what I need. It's not like Jerry isn't going to get any of the cake, but no! Jerry has to have juice. It's infuriating!

Tony: Anything else, Sandy?

Sandy: No.

Tony: Do you have questions for one another?

Jerry: Yeah. Why does Sandy have to be such a jerk?

Sandy: That's name-calling! You said you wouldn't call names!

Tony: We did agree to not call names, Jerry. Is there another way you can ask Sandy the question?

Jerry: Why is Sandy always acting like baking is the most important thing? Why can't I take the orange and make juice if I'm thirsty?

Tony: I don't know. Why don't you ask Sandy?

Sandy: I know that you want juice, but you want some of my Blue Ribbon Pound Cake, too. . . . If there's no orange peel, there's no Blue Ribbon Pound Cake. You just make me so mad when you come in and interrupt everything I have planned and take the orange just because you need juice. Blue Ribbon Pound Cakes don't grow on trees.

Jerry: You make great cakes, but when I come in all hot and thirsty, I really need my freshly squeezed orange juice. I can't wait to cut that orange open and squeeze the juice out of it.

Tony: Can you explain something to me? Sandy, how do you use the orange in your Blue Ribbon Pound Cake?

Sandy: I zest it.

Jerry: Oh, brother!

Sandy: That's what it's called. I have this thing like a little grater, and I rub it all over the orange peel and the peel comes off into the batter. It's what gives my Blue Ribbon Pound Cake that special something.

Tony: Thanks. And Jerry, how do you make juice?

Jerry: I cut the peel off and put the orange in the juicer.

Tony: Any ideas?

Sandy: Yes! If Jerry wants cake, then no juice for Jerry.

Jerry: That's just stupid. I'll make my juice, and you can dig the peel out of the trash for your stupid cake.

(There is a pause.)

Sandy: Better idea: I'll use the zest and when I'm done baking you can have the orange.

Jerry: I'm not waiting for you. When I come in I'm thirsty.

Tony: So what do we have so far? *(checks notes)* Sandy, you just need the peel, and Jerry, you just need the fruit.

Sandy: But I'm not digging the peel out of the trash.

Jerry: You wouldn't have to. I could leave it on the table for you. But I have to have my juice first.

Sandy: In other words, I have to wait for you to come back until I can finish my cake. This isn't working.

Tony: Wait a minute, Sandy. Is there some way that there could be juice ready when Jerry needed it and you wouldn't have to wait to start baking?

Sandy: I'm not making Jerry's juice, if that's what you mean.

Jerry: Just take the peel, and leave the fruit in the fridge. I'll make my own juice when I get home.

Tony: Will that work?

Sandy: Works for me.

Jerry: Will I still get some cake?

PRACTICE CASE #1:
NOISE FROM TWO CUBICLES DOWN

Lilly/Lyle and Martin/Martha are accounts receivable clerks. There are fifteen clerks in their department. All of them sit in cubicles and make calls reminding customers to submit payment.

In the six months that Lilly/Lyle has worked for the company, Lilly/Lyle has become the top bill collector in the department. Lilly/Lyle hits over 97 percent of Lilly's/Lyle's quota every month, while the department average is 92 percent. Martin/Martha has been in the department for three and a half years. Martin's/Martha's last review included praise for "your in-depth knowledge of the operation, your positive relationships with clients, and your professionalism."

Martin/Martha has a problem with Lilly/Lyle. Martin/Martha acknowledges that the other clerk gets results, but Lilly/Lyle tells jokes on the telephone and talks and laughs loudly. Martin/Martha finds this distracting. Martin's/Martha's approach with customers is quieter. Martin/Martha says that Lilly's/Lyle's lack of professionalism makes it hard to hear customers on the telephone.

"Sometimes," says Martin/Martha, "I can't even hear myself think."

Martin/Martha has talked with Lilly/Lyle about this on three separate occasions. Each time, Lilly/Lyle promised to be quieter. Martin/Martha says that Lilly/Lyle is quiet for a little while and then gets noisy again.

Lilly/Lyle is tired of Martin/Martha complaining about this. "I may be loud, but I get results."

Neither one of them wants to go to the manager about this. They are embarrassed about not being able to work it out. Besides, they do not want anyone to get in trouble.

Rita (or Ron), a friend from another department, recently attended a wonderful workshop called *The Conflict Management Skills Workshop*. Lilly/Lyle and Martin/Martha have asked Rita/Ron to help them work things out.

PRACTICE CASE #1: NOISE FROM TWO CUBICLES DOWN

Notes for Lilly/Lyle

You have been in the department for only six months and already you are the best collector the company has. For five of the six months, you have outperformed the department average by at least 5 percent.

You love your job and are proud of your success. The manager has told you that you have potential to move up in the company. "People have their eyes on you," were her exact words.

Although you have no accounting background, you are smart and can figure out most jobs. Your partner is a dentist, and you worked part-time in the dental practice as office manager. In fact, your current boss offered you a job after overhearing a collections call you made in the dentist's office. When you came to work, the manager said you were a natural and didn't need any training. "Here's your portfolio. I'm turning you loose," was all the manager ever said.

You feel that it would be inappropriate to mention to anyone else that you may be in line for a promotion. Although you want to get along with Martin/Martha, you will never do anything that might lower your productivity. You think Martin/Martha may be jealous of your success.

PRACTICE CASE #1:
NOISE FROM TWO CUBICLES DOWN

Notes for Martin/Martha

The last thing you want in the world is to have problems with anybody at work. You are usually very quiet and keep to yourself. You wouldn't even have spoken with Lilly/Lyle about this, except that it is very important to you.

In your three and a half years in the department, you have trained several people. You are pleased that one of your trainees has been promoted into management and another is doing well in payables. "At the end of the day," you tell your trainees, "the company lives or dies in accounts receivable."

Lilly/Lyle is the only new hire you haven't trained in more than two years. The other new hires usually came from business school or had some accounting or bookkeeping training. The only prior experience Lilly/Lyle had was working in a family dental practice as office manager. The manager said that she had seen Lilly/Lyle in action and that no training was necessary. "Here's your portfolio. I'm turning you loose," was all the manager ever said.

You are afraid that Lilly's/Lyle's success is beginner's luck, and that other new people will adopt the same loud, rambunctious style. You are also afraid that your numbers might start slipping. It is getting harder and harder to concentrate with all that noise coming from two cubicles down.

PRACTICE CASE #2:
THE BACKUP

Gina/Gene has been the only drill press operator on the third shift for seventeen years. Nobody ever needs to tell Gina/Gene what to do. As Gina/Gene says, "The work is there. The work gets done."

Over the years, Gina/Gene has become sort of a one-person department. Gina/Gene is always on time but takes breaks depending on the work flow. If it's a busy night, Gina/Gene works right through the break. If things are slow, Gina/Gene will go out on the loading dock for a smoke. "It all evens out in the end," says Gina/Gene.

Two weeks ago, the supervisor brought Claude/Claudette over to the drill press. Claude/Claudette, the supervisor said, is the new backup drill press operator. "In case we get busy or you get sick or something."

It is Gina's/Gene's responsibility to train Claude/Claudette. Claude/Claudette has been trained on newer equipment, but the old machine that Gina/Gene runs has its quirks.

At first Gina/Gene got along well with the new trainee. It was nice to have someone to talk to. The problem, according to Gina/Gene, is that there is only one workstation and there isn't enough to keep two people busy. So, while Claude/Claudette is running the drill press, Gina/Gene does setup work. When the setup work is done, Gina/Gene stands near the machine and makes comments on Claude's/Claudette's work.

Claude/Claudette is annoyed by this behavior. Gina/Gene has said that Claude/Claudette is doing a fine job but seems to feel that there is still a need to comment on everything the other worker does.

The supervisor insists that these two work together. He has sent them to Ted/Tania in human resources. Ted/Tania recently attended a workshop where they practiced problem solving and thinks this method might help the two drill press operators.

PRACTICE CASE #2:
THE BACKUP

Notes for Gina/Gene

You have worked third shift longer than anyone in the company. For seventeen years, you have run the drill press. Nobody can remember when anyone else has run that machine on graveyard. Everyone calls it Gina's/Gene's Machine.

You don't need supervision. You are used to setting your own pace and proud of the high-quality work that you put out. In the seventeen years you have run your machine, you have missed only eight days of work. One year, your picture was in the company's annual report. Your coworkers had the picture framed, and it is hanging on a post near your machine.

You can't see why they wanted to train a backup, but you just decided to "keep quiet and do what I was told." Claude/Claudette is a nice person and picked up the quirks of the old machine very quickly.

After about three weeks, there was no more need for training, but you still keep an eye on things. Once, several of Claude's/Claudette's pieces went out with a glaring mistake. The work was kicked back to your station. You feel that it reflected badly on you.

You know it bothers Claude/Claudette to have you watching all the time, but you aren't going to get into trouble because of someone else's mistakes.

Last week Claude/Claudette yelled at you to back off. You muttered an obscenity, and Claude/Claudette went to the supervisor. Now you have to go to a meeting in human resources to talk things out.

You don't know why there has to be a meeting, but you have decided to "keep quiet and do what I am told."

PRACTICE CASE #2: THE BACKUP

Notes for Claude/Claudette

Gina/Gene is driving you nuts. You feel like you can barely breathe the way Gina/Gene hovers while you work.

Gina/Gene has said that you run the drill press as well as anybody, but because of one time when you misread a work order, you can't get any peace. The work was sent back and you fixed it, but Gina/Gene continues to bring it up.

You like the job. The work is easy. When Gina/Gene is running the drill press, you sweep and do setup work. You used to read when things were really slow, but lately—just so Gina/Gene can see how it feels—you have been standing and watching while Gina/Gene works.

You are convinced that this has caused Gina/Gene to stand even closer to your machine while you are working. Last week, you lost your temper and yelled, "Get out of my face!"

You know that wasn't the correct way to handle things, but Gina/Gene made things even worse by cursing at you. You don't need to take that from anyone, so you told the supervisor.

Now the supervisor has told you that if you don't work things out, he will find someone who can. You are going to meet with Ted/Tania in human resources.

PRACTICE CASE #3: NEVER TALK TO ME THAT WAY AGAIN!

Leslie/Lorenzo is the vice president of sales for HowdyCard, a greeting card company. Tomás/Tammy heads up human resources. They have never seemed to get along very well.

None of Leslie's/Lorenzo's people have ever gone through Tomás's/Tammy's orientation program, and the only time they speak to one another is if there is a compensation question for one of the salespeople.

Tomás/Tammy presented a graph at the last executive council meeting that showed the percentage of compliance for attendance at the orientation program. The sales department was highlighted in brilliant red ink, as was the chart's title: "Zero Cooperation from Sales."

There was an uncomfortable pause when the slide went up. Finally, Leslie/ Lorenzo said, "I guess we were too busy having HowdyCard's best year ever to slow down and sit through orientation."

"A little cooperation would go a long way," countered Tomás/Tammy. "Everyone is tired of the arrogance of the salespeople. It's as if rules apply to everyone but them."

"Hey," said Leslie/Lorenzo, "the rule is that training programs are discretionary by department. Maybe if the orientation weren't so boring, people would want to go to it without me putting a gun to their head. Anyway, salespeople would rather be making money than wasting it."

Now Tomás/Tammy was really angry. "It's people like you who will keep this company from ever moving beyond the status quo."

Leslie/Lorenzo sat quietly and seethed for a moment, then said, "That's it," and left the meeting.

Tomás/Tammy has asked Barry/Beryl, a business professor at the local community college, to help them work this out. After several tries, Barry/Beryl reached Leslie/Lorenzo on the telephone.

"I'll come to the meeting," said Leslie/Lorenzo, "but Tomás/Tammy can never talk to me that way again."

PRACTICE CASE #3: NEVER TALK TO ME THAT WAY AGAIN!

Notes for Tomás/Tammy

As head of human resources at HowdyCard, you have worked hard to make important changes in the company. Your new-hire orientation program has helped people to feel comfortable as they start work in the hectic and creative atmosphere of the greeting card business. You are convinced that this program is a major reason why employee attrition is at an all-time low.

You had to sell the orientation program to your colleagues over a period of one year. At first, nobody would listen. When you started receiving rave reviews for the program, people started attending one department at a time.

Now people don't know what they did without the program. It is a major feather in your cap.

You are offended that Leslie/Lorenzo and the sales department don't take the services that your group provides more seriously. You are also worried that sales will become out of step with the culture of the company. This could cause factions to form.

Leslie/Lorenzo never even responded to your message to meet about orientation. The sales group also goes around your department and does its own recruiting. The last straw for you was when Leslie/Lorenzo went outside of the company for sales training even though your training manager was formerly the sales trainer at your biggest competitor.

PRACTICE CASE #3:
NEVER TALK TO ME THAT WAY AGAIN!

Notes for Leslie/Lorenzo

You have been heading up sales for HowdyCard for three years. Sales numbers have increased by more than 35 percent for each year that you have been at the helm. You use your instincts to make hiring and other business decisions, and you don't want human resources to get in the way of your or the company's success.

You keep meetings and training to a minimum and it is working well for you. You tell your salespeople, "If you aren't selling, you're not making money for yourself or the company. If you're not making money for yourself, why are you coming to work? If you're not making money for the company, why are we letting you come to work?"

You want human resources out of your hair. You even sent some of your people to an outside training class even though you know the training manager of the human resources department used to do sales training for your biggest competitor.

The only reason you have agreed to meet with Tomás/Tammy and Barry/Beryl is that you think you may have overly avoided training classes and that you may start looking uncooperative in the eyes of the CEO.

You would be willing to give training a try if it could be scheduled around the busy days of your salespeople, but you aren't going to even talk to Tomás/Tammy at the meeting unless you hear a sincere apology.

PRACTICE CASE #4:
MY OLD FRIEND IS MY NEW BOSS

Doug/Dolores and Kay/Ken have worked at the jewelry counter at York's Department Store since graduating from high school four years ago. They did not know one another very well in high school, but during the time they have worked together, they have become good friends. They are both on the company softball team and sometimes get together outside of work.

Last week the section manager, Xina Henderson, quit. Both Doug/Dolores and Kay/Ken applied for Xina's job. The operations manager said it was a tough decision between two good workers, but he picked Doug/Dolores. What influenced the choice the most, he said, was that Doug/Dolores has been attending college business classes on Wednesday nights.

The manager told Kay/Ken, "If you want to get ahead, you should take a page out of Doug's/Dolores's book."

Kay/Ken is working the jewelry counter alone until Doug/Dolores finds a replacement. Kay/Ken was late for work on Doug's/Dolores's first day as section manager. In the past, if one of the two friends was late, the other one would work alone to set up the register and the displays in time for opening. When the first customers arrived that particular morning, the jewelry counter was not ready for business.

Doug/Dolores told Kay/Ken that lateness is unacceptable even though they are friends. Doug/Dolores stopped by the jewelry counter before Kay's/Ken's lunch break to see if they could eat together. Kay/Ken said, "There's nothing that says I have to eat with the boss."

Since then, the two friends have spoken only when they had to. Kay/Ken has started to call in sick every Monday. Doug/Dolores is worried that the excessive absences may get Kay/Ken in trouble and stopped by to talk about it. Doug/Dolores said, "If you've got a problem, boss, write me up."

Nguyen/Nora, who works in the cafeteria, has just finished a workshop called *The Conflict Management Skills Workshop*. After listening to Kay/Ken complain about Doug/Dolores, Nguyen/Nora has convinced the two friends to sit down together to try to work things out. They have agreed to meet in the training room after closing.

PRACTICE CASE #4: MY OLD FRIEND IS MY NEW BOSS

Notes for Doug/Dolores

Kay/Ken is your best friend. You are worried because Kay/Ken is nearly out of sick days, and you may have to do a write-up if these Monday absences continue. The absences also add to your workload and make you look bad to your boss. This makes you angry. You expected better performance from your friend.

You think one thing that is bothering Kay/Ken is that you were both planning on buying a Jet Ski together until you decided to spend money to go to night classes.

You had a brief argument about the Jet Ski, and you thought it was over. Now the manager has made a big deal out of you being promoted instead of Kay/Ken because you are taking classes. You are certain this has added fuel to the fire.

PRACTICE CASE #4:
MY OLD FRIEND IS MY NEW BOSS

Notes for Kay/Ken

Doug/Dolores is your best friend. In the old days, you would cover for one another. Now you feel that Doug/Dolores is going by the book too much.

You are angry and feel like your friend has abandoned you. Last year, the two of you saved up to buy a Jet Ski together, and then Doug/Dolores decided to spend money on night classes instead.

Now the manager can't stop talking about how Doug/Dolores is leadership material because of the classes.

You came in late on Doug's/Dolores's first day and things have gone downhill since then. You don't want to lose your friend or your job, but you don't know what to do. You have been looking at the help-wanted advertisements on Sundays and calling in sick on Mondays so that you can go to interviews. You're afraid that if the "new" Doug/Dolores finds out, you will be fired.

PRACTICE CASE #5:
R-E-S-P-E-C-T

Hien/Hanna and Paloma/Pete work together at the Crown Cab & Limo Co. dispatch office. Paloma/Pete supervises Hien/Hanna and two other dispatchers. Crown Cab has a regular street cab service and also rents limousines.

Recently, the company has begun chartering buses to pick up large groups of conventiongoers at the airport. The company not only provides the buses but also has a crew of greeters who hold up signs for the incoming clients and direct them through baggage claim and onto the buses. A large meeting may have more than a thousand people arriving during a twelve-hour period.

When the company has a convention coming into town, Paloma/Pete goes to the airport to supervise the greeters and to ensure that everything goes smoothly. In Paloma/Pete's absence, Hien/Hanna takes over supervisory duties at dispatch.

Paloma/Pete is worried that the new supervisor duties may be too much for Hien/Hanna to handle. Hien/Hanna seems curt when talking to drivers, and the other two dispatchers complain that Hien/Hanna yells at them.

Paloma/Pete asked Hien/Hanna about this change in behavior. Hien/Hanna said, "I'm tired of the way you disrespect me and continually undermine my authority." Paloma/Pete doesn't understand what Hien/Hanna is talking about but is afraid to talk about it further because Hien/Hanna has a reputation for yelling when angry.

"I can put up with a lot," says Paloma/Pete, "but if Hien/Hanna yells at me, I know I'm going to lose my temper."

Crown Cab is two doors down from the community mediation center. Paloma/Pete asked Olga/Omar from the center to see whether Hien/Hanna would agree to a meeting.

"I think it's a waste of time," says Hien/Hanna, "but I'll try anything to make working with Paloma/Pete better."

PRACTICE CASE #5:
R-E-S-P-E-C-T

Notes for Paloma/Pete

You work hard and you are tired. The company is growing and you now have to not only run the dispatch office, but you supervise the new airport crews as well. You enjoy the excitement and the pressure to some extent, but there are downsides. You don't feel as if your salary has kept up with your responsibilities. You also have an eight-year-old daughter who usually stays with you every other weekend. You have missed the last two weekends. You feel as if you are not being a very good parent, and your ex is beginning to lose patience.

Now on top of all this, Hien/Hanna is acting strangely. You don't know whether it is the pressure, but this usually outstanding worker is complaining to everyone who will listen that you are somehow disrespectful.

On your way past Hien's/Hanna's desk the other day, you asked what the problem is. Hien/Hanna said, "I'm tired of the way you disrespect me and continually undermine my authority."

You were in a hurry to get to the airport, and you didn't want to start an argument, so you left without saying anything more. You have asked Olga/Omar, a volunteer at the local community mediation center, to help. Hien/Hanna has reluctantly agreed to come to a meeting.

PRACTICE CASE #5:
R-E-S-P-E-C-T

Notes for Hien/Hanna

You work hard as a dispatcher and you are tired. The company is growing and you now have the added responsibility of supervising the other dispatchers when Paloma/Pete is away.

You enjoy the excitement and the pressure to some extent, but there are downsides. You don't feel like your salary has kept up with your responsibilities. You also like to work out at the gym three evenings a week and play in an adult soccer league on Saturdays. Lately, your work schedule has been keeping you away from the gym. Last Saturday, you were late for a match. You are afraid that if you start missing soccer matches and practices, the coach may ask you to step aside for another player.

Now on top of all this, Paloma/Pete is acting strangely. You don't know whether it is the pressure, but you used to like this boss. Now suddenly, you are being treated with disrespect. Paloma/Pete shouts incomplete instructions at you on the way out the door. If you don't get the instructions right, Paloma/Pete corrects you in front of everybody else.

As if this weren't bad enough, when you give the other dispatchers instructions, they often will not follow them. A typical response is, "That's not what Paloma/Pete told me to do." How can you possibly supervise the dispatchers without Paloma's/Pete's support?

Paloma/Pete and somebody from the community mediation center have asked you to come to a meeting. You don't think anyone can get through to Paloma/Pete, but you decide to go if it will help to keep the peace.

TWO SIBLINGS AND ONE ORANGE—TAKE TWO: TRANSFORMATIVE MEDIATION SCRIPT

People:

Mediator—Tony
Sibling 1—Jerry
Sibling 2—Sandy

A table and several chairs are available. As the siblings come in, Tony greets them and asks them to take a seat. They sit where they choose. When both siblings are seated, Tony takes a seat.

Tony: How can I help you?

Jerry: We're here because of Sandy. We have one orange in the house. This jerk knows that I need it, and . . .

Sandy: (interrupting) That's exactly like Jerry! Everything is about what *Jerry* needs. . . .

Jerry: Will you listen to this hysteria! It should be pretty easy for you to figure out what we need to do here.

Tony: (interrupting) Let's wait just a minute, Jerry. Sandy, you too. You need to figure out how I can help you with this. I'm not here to make any decisions for you. This isn't like court where you tell me things and I decide for you. This is an opportunity for the two of you to sit down together, and really listen to one another as you talk about what's going on with the orange. How does that sound?

Jerry: I have a solution in mind already. We just have to get through to Simple Simon over there.

Tony: Right now I need to know that you are both willing to listen to one another. For now, tell me if you are willing to talk this out.

Jerry: Sure. I'll stay if Sandy stays.

Tony: Sandy?

Sandy: I'll stay, but Jerry has to stop calling me Simple Simon.

Tony: Does that work for you, Jerry?

Jerry: Sure.

Tony: Okay. *(writing)* "Jerry won't call Sandy Simple Simon."

Sandy: Or any other name!

Tony: Shall we make that a rule for going forward?

The siblings nod their agreement.

Tony: How does this sound? Everything you tell me will be confidential. I won't tell anyone about what we talk about here unless you want me to. You may see me take notes so I can keep my thinking straight, but you'll also see me tear my notes up when we are finished. I won't take sides but will be here to be sure that you both are represented and to help you find out what is truly important to one another. Sound good?

Sandy and Jerry nod.

Tony: Who would like to go first?

Sandy: It may as well be Jerry. Jerry always goes first.

Jerry: All right, I will.

Tony: Is that really all right, Sandy?

Sandy: Yeah.

Jerry: Sandy has this self-image of being a great chef or something. I came home from running and wanted some fresh orange juice. It's full of antioxidants and vitamin C. I need it after a run, but—no! Sandy has to bake. I'm hot, I'm tired, I'm thirsty. So all I did was pick up the orange and start to walk out of the room. . . .

Sandy: I was using it!

Jerry: See how Sandy always interrupts and yells? Anyway, I picked up the orange. . . .

Sandy: I do not interrupt and yell!

Tony: Jerry?

Jerry: I picked up the orange and started to go out of the room and Sandy came after me screaming that the orange wasn't mine, that it was part of some recipe.

(There is a pause.)

Tony: Anything else, Jerry?

Jerry: That's about all there was to it. All I wanted was to make some orange juice.

Sandy: I was using that orange! Jerry just waltzes in and grabs the orange without asking, and I need the entire peel to grate into my special Blue Ribbon Pound Cake. It's just like Jerry to ignore what I need. It's not like Jerry isn't going to get any of the cake, but no! Jerry has to have juice. It's infuriating!

Tony: Anything else, Sandy?

Sandy: No.

Tony: Do you have questions for one another?

Jerry: Yeah. Why does Sandy have to be such a jerk?

Sandy: That's name-calling! You said you wouldn't call names!

Tony: We did agree to not call names, Jerry. Is there another way you can ask Sandy the question?

Jerry: Why is Sandy always acting like baking is the most important thing? Why can't I take the orange and make juice if I'm thirsty?

Tony: I don't know. Why don't you ask Sandy?

Sandy: I know that you want juice, but you want some of my Blue Ribbon Pound Cake, too. . . . If there's no orange peel, there's no Blue Ribbon Pound Cake. You just make me so mad when you come in and interrupt everything I have planned and take the orange just because you need juice. Blue Ribbon Pound Cakes don't grow on trees.

Jerry: You make great cakes, but when I come in all hot and thirsty, I really need my freshly squeezed orange juice. I can't wait to cut that orange open and squeeze the juice out of it.

Tony: Sandy, I think that Jerry has said something that you may want to hear. Jerry, what do you think about Sandy's cakes?

Jerry: I think they're great. You can be a real pain, sometimes, but your cakes are the best.

Sandy: Then, why can't you let me use the orange when I need it?

Tony: Please wait, Sandy. Did you hear Jerry talk about your baking?

Sandy: What?

Tony: Jerry?

Jerry: You're an excellent baker.

Sandy: Wow. Thanks. You always seem to be making fun of my baking. If you like my baking so much, why couldn't you see that I needed the orange?

Jerry: I didn't know you needed the orange. I really needed orange juice after my run. You know the electrolytes . . .

Sandy: Right. And the vitamin C.

Jerry: That's right. And the vitamin C. This is very important to me.

Sandy: I know.

There is an uncomfortable silence.

Tony: What else?

Jerry: Sometimes Sandy gets excited and interrupts, but it's really not a problem.

Tony: It doesn't bother you?

Jerry: Well, yes, but I know that when I get excited I call Sandy Simple Simon.

Sandy: That has to stop, no matter what.

Jerry: I'll be more careful.

Sandy: More careful might not be good enough. It really bothers me when you call me names.

Jerry: Well, then don't be so stupid about whether or not I can make orange juice.

Sandy: Well, maybe you should open your eyes and see that I'm baking and I have everything laid out that I need. Everything—including the only orange in the house.

Jerry: I can't read your mind, Sandy!

Sandy: You know how I bake. Just pay attention once in a while and you would know that if an orange is on the counter with all of my stuff, I'm going to use it. All you think about is what you need at the moment.

Jerry: Well, all you think about is what you need to bake your stupid cakes!

Tony: Jerry, what do you think about Sandy's baking?

Jerry: I know. Sandy's cakes are great. I meant that. But there are other things in life.

Tony: Can you think of a way to tell Sandy what you mean without starting a fight?

Jerry: (*after a pause*) Not really.

Tony: Sandy, what would work for you?

Sandy: I think Jerry likes my cakes but thinks that's all I have in my life. Jerry is wrong. There are many things about me that people don't know.

Jerry: I know what you mean. Sometimes people say that all I do is run.

LISTENING PRACTICE OBSERVATION SHEET

While the first person tells a story, listen carefully and jot down some key phrases in the box on the left. When the story is repeated, make note of how well the content and emotion are retold.

Key Phrases:

1st Telling	Retelling

Content:
Notes:

Accurate?

[   ]   [   ]
yes   no

Emotion:
Notes:

Accurate?

[   ]   [   ]
yes   no

Body Language:
Notes:

Accurate?

[   ]   [   ]
yes   no

LISTENING

Listening is the most important skill that we can develop to improve our ability to make conflict productive. We need to ensure that we are focused on what the other person is saying so that we can make good decisions about how we will respond. We need to be certain that communication—the words and actions being presented—flows in every possible direction, and that we are receptive and responsive to everything that is going on.

LISTEN FOR CONTENT

One of the things we need to listen for is content. What is it that the other person is saying? Are you good at listening and remembering what you just heard? Can you listen to a half hour of evening news and then tell someone what was covered, or do you zone out on the couch and catch only odd bits of information?

Try these exercises: Watch the evening news and take notes. Then recap the day's top stories during the last commercial break and see whether your version matches the announcer's recap. You can also do this with a partner. You each take notes and compare them when the program is over. What did you think was important enough to write down? Is that different from what your partner recorded? Do this exercise for a week or so, and see whether you can remember more while taking fewer and fewer notes. Learn your own style for listening and remembering.

One way to determine whether you understand what people are telling you is to repeat it back to them. Ask them whether you got it right: "So you think that we should look at the way we listen to each other, right?" Give them a chance to respond, and listen to the response. They will let you know whether you have it right or not.

LISTEN FOR CONTEXT

Another thing we need to listen for is context. This is everything other than content. It is the big box that content comes to us in. Context may include emotion, the culture of the speaker, the culture of the company, or the speaker's rank in the company relative to yours or to others in the room.

We listen for context not only with our ears but with our eyes and our intuition as well. We also listen for context through a filter of our own beliefs and biases.

If we know what our beliefs and biases are, we can acknowledge them and temporarily put them aside while we listen. (See Handout 3.2: Looking Neutral.)

TIPS FOR FOCUSED LISTENING

It can be difficult to focus while we are listening. Your ears are working, but so is everything else. It is as if there is some kind of traffic jam in your brain. One solution is to fight to keep your mind clear of distractions. Some people will focus on the speaker's lips and words, mentally repeating what is said to keep themselves on track. Although this works well sometimes, a better method may be not to fight our brain's tendency to split its attention.

Either we can acknowledge that there is a lot going on in our brain and make room for one more thing, or we can move the other stuff aside to create a prime spot for what is happening at the moment that we need to be listening to.

Our bodies are like huge clusters of antennae that constantly collect information and send it to our brains. This is good news for us as we send and receive complex messages. The problem is that the signals we want to focus on compete with everything else going on, and with everything else that has ever gone on, and is stored up there in our heads. The brain can be a very noisy place.

You can't fight it, so learn to live with it. You can practice the *A-1, B-2* exercise to help you allow the other information to continue to flow while focusing on what is important at the moment. You will also build your skill to focus while your brain is processing a myriad of information, and you will become better at making decisions about how to respond to what you are experiencing.

REFLECTION WORKSHEET: CHOOSING ACTIONS

We have been talking about "fight or flight." No matter which choice you make, there are advance signals your body sends out that you can use to know that you are about to become aggressive or back down.

Think about these three questions and jot down some thoughts to talk about.

What are some things you feel in your body when you are frightened?

What are some things you feel in your body when you are about to lose your temper?

Do you have ways of calming your body so that you can think more clearly when you are in a conflict situation? What are some of them?

TIPS FOR CALM LISTENING

We sometimes try to focus on listening by talking to our brain as if it were a pesky pet: "Not now, brain. I'm listening!" The harder we push against our brain's tendency to switch from one topic to another, the harder it seems to push back: "But you mustn't forget to pick up your dry cleaning tomorrow!"

A way to calm your brain is to make a promise to it. Keep a pad of paper near you while you are listening, and write notes to yourself as stray thoughts pop into your head. This will keep your brain happy and it won't bring up the topic again for a while. It's true you won't be listening 100 percent while you jot down "dry cleaning, Tues., PM," but you will be distracted for a shorter period of time by this than by trying to seesaw between telling your brain to pipe down and focusing on what you want to be listening to. The trick here is to not only take notes on what is being said to you, but to separately jot down your distractions. Promise your brain you'll get back to it later.

One approach for managing the traffic in your brain is to turn down the volume on everything except what is happening at the moment. This is difficult or even impossible to do if you try to force your brain to behave. Instead, think of your brain as a flowing river full of fascinating objects. Pick up the objects you are interested in at the moment, and let the other ones flow by. They will be back when you need them.

Try closing your eyes and sitting quietly before a meeting or conversation that you think will require calm listening. Have you ever noticed your own breath? Try not to make yourself breathe at any particular rate; merely observe your breathing. When you breathe in, say, "Breathe in" to yourself; when you breathe out, say, "Breathe out." It takes a little practice, but focusing on your breath will seem to clear your mind of everything else. Notice three breaths in a row and open your eyes. The next thing you see or hear will take a prime position in your mind.

If you notice yourself being distracted while someone is speaking, try noticing three breaths. Feel yourself breathe and think, "Breathe in, breathe out," with each cycle. You won't be listening to the other person for the ten seconds this takes, but when you tune back in, you will be absolutely focused. (You weren't listening anyway, and this simple exercise will clear your mind more quickly than trying to say, "Down, boy!" to your brain or emotions.)

Here is a list of simple tools that will help you to stay focused while listening. Pick the one that you are most comfortable with, or use them all in combination.

Tools for Staying Focused While Listening

1. Take notes of what the speaker is saying—and check to see whether you are getting it right.

2. Train yourself to multitrack—"A-1, B-2, C-3, . . . " It will help you to become accustomed to sorting through all the signals to focus on the one you want.

3. Take notes on what is distracting you—and promise your brain that you will get back to it.

4. Calm your mind. If you're not listening well anyway, take a ten-second break and notice three breaths. You'll listen better when you "come back."

ACTION PLAN

1. What Should We Do?

Consider everything you know about conflict and write three reasonable things your workshop group can do to make conflict a positive experience for the company.

A.

B.

C.

2. Why Is That So Important?

Make a one- or two-sentence business case and/or a one- or two-sentence personal case for each of the three things you have listed.

A.

B.

C.

LEVEL ONE EVALUATION

Today's Date: _____

Thank you for the opportunity to serve you with this program. Your opinions and ideas are extremely valuable. Through your feedback, we can continually improve this and other training courses. Please be honest and constructive. Thank you—we value your thoughts and suggestions.

Please circle the number that most accurately represents your thoughts. Please comment on any item.

1   Unsatisfactory—Did Not Meet My Expectations
2   Fair—Met Some of My Expectations
3   Good—Met My Expectations
4   Very Good—Exceeded Some of My Expectations
5   Excellent—Exceeded All of My Expectations

   1. Logistics of training session:

      a. Meeting room facilities   1 2 3 4 5

      b. Dates and times   1 2 3 4 5

    Comments:

   2. Overall information presented   1 2 3 4 5

    Comments:

3. Facilitator's knowledge and expertise   1   2   3   4   5

Comments:

4. Facilitator's interaction with group   1   2   3   4   5

Comments:

Please rate the discussion and activities of the following topic sections in terms of how useful you found them to be in helping to improve or enhance your conflict skills.

1   Not Useful
2   Less Useful
3   Useful
4   More Useful
5   Very Useful

5. Naming the Workshop   1   2   3   4   5

Comments:

6. Ways of Seeing   1   2   3   4   5

Comments:

7. Stories about taking a second look   1   2   3   4   5

Comments:

8. Ways of Seeing Conflict (Win, Lose, or Draw/Even,   1   2   3   4   5
Bigger, Different)

   Comments:

9. Two Sisters and One Orange   1   2   3   4   5

   Comments:

10. Reflection Sheets   1   2   3   4   5

   Comments:

11. Party Time Discussion and Debates   1   2   3   4   5

   Comments:

12. Mediation Practice   1   2   3   4   5

   Comments:

13. My Personal Conflict Strategy   1   2   3   4   5

   Comments:

14. Action Planning/Group Conflict Strategy   1 2 3 4 5

    Comments:

15. What topic/discussion was of the most value to you?:
    Please explain:

16. What topic/discussion was of the least value to you?
    Please explain:

17. **General Comments**

Thanks!

STORIES

229

Story 1.10: *My Dad and the Last Brownie*
         When people own the problem, they own the solution.
Story 1.11: *Rueben and Laurel*
Story 1.12: *Two Sisters, One Orange*
Story 3.1:   *The Leaf Blower*

TO BAG OR NOT TO BAG

I grew up in southern California and now live in the Philadelphia area. In southern California, when you go to the grocery store, the checker or some-one else from the store will put your groceries in the bag for you. It doesn't matter whether you are in a fancy store or not. In Philadelphia, until recently, the custom has been for customers to put their own groceries in the bag. I have lived in Philly for ten years. On a recent trip to San Diego, I went with a friend to the supermarket.

As the checker began to ring up our food, I moved to the end of the checkout counter, grabbed a bag, and started to put my groceries away. It seemed to me to be a perfectly normal thing to do. The checker stopped checking, and my friend's mouth fell open. Neither spoke, until the checker said, "Is everything okay?"

It's all she could think of to say, since she had to be polite to the customer, and since my behavior was so bizarre.

"Is everything okay?"

I was just as startled. Nothing else came to mind, so I apologized. "Sorry," I said, and quickly took a step away from the groceries.

Everything went back to normal—the "right" way for these people on the other coast—and when the checker was finished ringing up the order, she put the food into bags for us. As she was bagging, I explained that where I come from people bag their own groceries, and my friend and the checker shook their heads and clucked sympathetically.

The truth, I think, is that one way is not morally superior to the other. Some people may like to bag their own groceries, while others may not. It might only be what they get used to. We certainly weren't going to have a conflict about it, but sometimes, customs are exactly what we fight about.

GOOD MANNERS

A Saudi businessperson was furious because the CEO of the company he was coming to visit in the United States did not meet him at the airport. It ruined the trip and strained relations between the two companies. The U.S. CEO thought that the Saudi visitor would want to go to his hotel and relax or freshen up before meeting anyone.

Even after a North American explained that it was common for U.S. businesspeople to make their own way from the airport to their meetings, the guest could not get over his impression that he was dealing with extremely rude people.

Can you think of instances when customs or rules that might not matter in the larger picture have been misunderstood and caused problems for you? Remember, this doesn't have to be between people from different countries or different coasts. It can be equally confusing between people who live together or who work together.

THE LILLIPUTIAN EGG WARS

". . . the primitive way of breaking eggs before we eat them, was upon the larger end: but his present Majesty's grandfather, while he was a boy, going to eat an egg, and breaking it according to the ancient practice, happened to cut one of his fingers. Whereupon the Emperor, his father published an edict, commanding all his subjects, upon great penalties, to break the smaller end of their eggs. The people so highly resented this law, that our histories tell us there have been six rebellions raised on that account; wherein one emperor lost his life, and another his crown. These civil commotions were constantly fomented by the monarchs of Blefuscu [a neighboring and rival kingdom]; and when they were quelled, the exiles always fled for refuge to that empire. It is computed, that eleven thousand persons have, at several times, suffered death, rather than submit to break their eggs at the smaller end. Many hundred large volumes have been published upon this controversy: but the books of the Big-Endians have been long forbidden, and the whole party rendered incapable by law of holding employments. During the course of these troubles, the emperors of Blefuscu did frequently expostulate by their ambassadors, accusing us of making a schism in religion, by offending against a fundamental doctrine of our great prophet Lustrog, in the fifty-fourth chapter of the *Brundecral*. . . . This, however, is thought to be a mere strain upon the text: for the words are these; *That all true believers shall break their eggs at the convenient end* . . ."

—From *Gulliver's Travels* by Jonathan Swift, 1726

THE FARMER ON THE PORCH

There is an old story that I heard when I was a kid about a reporter who was driving through the southern United States. I don't know whether you have ever been in the Deep South, but it is beautiful country. This man was driving on an old red-dirt road, winding his way through a grove of trees. Here and there he would pass a little farm or deserted filling station. It was hot and humid and buggy—the kind of day that makes you want to sit as still as you can in the shade with a tall glass of cold lemonade.

Our reporter was looking for something to write about—a bit of local color. He drove past a little house—no paint on the gray boards, sagging roof, and an old man tipped back in his chair on the weather-beaten front porch. The old man was rocking gently in the heat and had attached a long wooden pole to a garden hoe. This invention allowed the old man to rock on the porch and hoe his garden at the same time.

The reporter smiled. "A lazy day in the Old South," he thought. He had his local color. The story goes that as the reporter drove by, something made him look in his side mirror for one last picture. That is when he noticed that the old man had no legs.

A second look turned what would have been a patronizing story about a stereotype into a story of courage, strength, and indomitable will.

ès

What the reporter saw the first time was true. He had seen it for himself. If we knew this reporter to be reliable and he hadn't looked back, we would have believed the truth of his first story. What the reporter saw when he looked back was true. He had seen it for himself. If we choose to believe the reporter, then this becomes true.

Often, what makes what we see hold different truths is the meaning we decide to put on it. When we add the layers of meaning that come from our customs, beliefs, and experience, the story becomes more or less true for us.

If one of us had seen one story and another had seen the other, we might even have something to fight about.

THE PINK MOMENT

Things can be different depending upon where you are standing, and even what you choose to look at. I grew up in southern California. For some reason, many people in the rest of the United States think that Californians are a little strange. Some of us are.

Just north of Los Angeles in the hills overlooking the Pacific Ocean is the town of Ojai. Ojai, California, is a pretty little place that has attracted artists and creative types since the end of the 1800s. It has been a while since I've been there, so I don't know if they still wait for the Pink Moment, but when I was there last, people were still proud of an interesting local tradition.

When the sun sets over the Pacific, people in Ojai wander outside. Stores shut down, or at least all work stops for awhile. Everybody is outside to watch the sun go down. It is beautiful, but a funny thing separates the locals from the visitors. People who are from Ojai come outside for the sunset, but as soon as the sun touches the edge of the ocean, they all turn their backs on it.

Anybody know why?

The Pink Moment, of course. When the sun is going down in Ojai, people who want to see the Pink Moment turn away from the sunset and watch the foothills to the east turn from green or gold to a faint, flickering rose.

THE COLORED BALL

Imagine that there is a huge ball suspended in the middle of the room. This side of the ball is red. This side of the ball is blue. If we had a class discussion about the ball, and I asked someone from this side of the room what color the ball is, she would say, "red." If I asked someone from this side of the room, he would say, "blue." If I spun the ball very fast, someone might say, "When the ball sits still, it is red (or blue, if you are one of *those* people) and when it spins, it is purple."

How could someone on the blue side convince someone on the red side that the blue side is right?

Have them come over to see this side.

And what happens if someone from one side goes over to the other side to get them to come over?

They see what is true for the other side.

Right. And the next challenge for this person who has seen both sides of the ball is to convince everybody else on both sides that things may be different depending upon where you are standing.

THE BLIND MEN AND THE ELEPHANT

One more story about how we can be convinced of competing truths . . . Anybody ever hear of the story of the blind men and the elephant? The story is about five blind friends who decide to learn about the elephant—a creature that they had heard of but that they had never experienced firsthand. The five split up to find out what they could about the elephant and then came back to meet and compare notes.

"The elephant," said the first blind man, "is very much like a snake."

"No," said the second. "The elephant is very much like a rope."

The other friends had different replies. One said an elephant is like a large leaf, another said it was like the trunk of a tree, and the last one said that the elephant is like an immense wall.

&

Of course, we know that one was feeling the trunk, another the tail, another the ear, and so on. In the story, the blind men get into a terrible fight.

How could they have avoided this?

By talking with one another. By listening. Etc.

Each blind man in the story had become a specialist on one part of the elephant and refused to acknowledge that there may be something that he did not know.

His perspective was determined by where he began and ended his experience.

All of the blind men were right. Together, if they figured out how to learn from one another, they would have also been right—and they would have benefited from their differing viewpoints to know more about elephants than any single one of them could by acting alone.

Does this ever happen in business?

What can we do about it?

What happens if the guy who thinks an elephant is like a leaf is the boss?

LOSING SARA

Four good friends—Sara, Art, Mihi, and Margaret—went into business together. Art was good at encouraging people to work well together and had the most business experience, so it was decided that he would head things up. Sara liked doing research, so tracking the competition and designing new products became her job. Margaret was highly energetic and well-liked by clients. She became the salesperson. Mihi had marketing experience and was very detail-oriented. She took over creating sales materials and keeping everyone and everything on track.

Their meetings were interesting, to say the least. Margaret and Art liked to talk a lot. The two of them would often monopolize the meetings, excitedly interrupting one another with their ideas. They were funny and enjoyed one another's company. Mihi would join in the joking but otherwise kept quiet during the meetings. She would take notes and occasionally interject to sum things up or move things along. It was the most difficult for Sara. Her office was in another city, and she would join the meetings by telephone. Nobody could see her and she had trouble knowing what was going on during the meetings.

Sara would usually call into the meetings with some carefully thought-out plan. When she presented her idea, Art would open things up for discussion. He and Margaret would then springboard one idea off another one until the plan didn't look a thing like what Sara had presented. Because she was naturally quieter than Margaret and Art, and because she had to telephone in to the meetings, Sara often felt as if her ideas weren't being heard.

When Art and Margaret would take Sara's ideas to the most extreme level, Mihi would remind them that time was almost up and that there were other things that needed to be talked about that day.

One day, Sara dropped a bombshell at the weekly meeting. She waited until the roundtable at the end of the session. This was a time when Art would go around to each person and ask how she thought the meeting had gone. Usually, people would say something like, "Great! I think we have generated a lot of good ideas today."

At this particular roundtable, Margaret had gone first. She thanked everybody for their help with a sales proposal that she had in front of a new client and said how much fun it was to work with people who cared so much about one another.

Art added that the best thing about their work together was that they all got along so well and loved to collaborate on creative solutions. Then, he asked Sara to take her turn at the roundtable.

Sara hesitated and took a deep breath. Her voice over the telephone sounded tight. "You know how important this business and all of you are to me," she said, "but I need you to know that as of the end of the month, I'll be leaving our company." Sara went on to say that she had already contacted the company's attorney to clarify the process of rescinding her partnership shares, and that she wanted her departure to be amicable.

The rest of the team was stunned. Finally, Art spoke. "Sara, please don't rush into anything. I'm sure that we can work out whatever is bothering you. Why don't you fly up here so that we can talk face-to-face?"

Margaret's eyes teared up. "I know it's been hard being so far away, Sara. I'm sure we can work things out if we all get together."

Sara answered quietly.

"I have been thinking about this for some time and even talked it over a little with Mihi. Most of the company's stuff is already packed up to ship back to you. I need to work with people I can see. I know this is for the best."

Margaret and Art tried to get Sara to give them a reason for quitting. Mihi busied herself with her notepad. Finally, the call came to an uncomfortable end with Sara promising to think about it and agreeing to talk with Art by telephone later in the week.

When they got off the telephone, Art turned to Mihi.

"Mihi?"

"All she ever told me was that she needed her ideas to be more respected. I said she needed to speak up around you two or else just do her own thing and hope you guys went along."

Margaret didn't want to talk. She said she was too upset.

Art told his two partners that he was going for a walk, got his coat, and left.

ঌ

There is a lot going on with these people. One thing that may be getting in the way of the four friends is the different way that each of them processes information. People learn in a variety of ways that may change depending upon the specific situation in which they find themselves.

Art, for example, waits for someone else's good idea then manipulates it. He bounces ideas off Margaret or anyone else who will join in until he is comfortable with what he has learned. Then he goes "outside the box," thinking of extreme variations on what he understands from the original proposal. He has fun doing this and doesn't particularly care what comes of it. One thing that Art knows for certain is that his way works for him. When the brainstorming session is over, there will always be more good ideas than he knows what to do with.

Margaret follows Art's lead and enjoys seeing him work. She sometimes wishes he would slow down. She thinks that some good ideas may be left in the dust if they move too quickly. Days after the meeting, Art is still coming up with new approaches. Margaret teases him about it, since she and the others have usually moved on to something else.

"Earth to Art" is a common joke among the four partners.

Margaret learns by testing and revising Art's ideas until they become practical. She does this quickly and then tells Mihi about it. Mihi figures out the potential costs and other details and tries to explain Margaret's results to the others.

Art and Margaret care deeply about their friends and feel terrible about what they see as their failure with Sara. They know they need Sara's careful planning and analysis to get things done. Sara enjoys her partners' energy but worries about how unmethodical they are. She would like, for a change, to be able to present an idea fully before Art takes off on his flights of fancy. Sara's quiet nature makes long-distance communication with her more outgoing colleagues that much more difficult.

Nobody seems to notice that Sara carefully studies several approaches and probable outcomes before presenting her ideas. Often, Art and Margaret come up with ideas that Sara has already analyzed and discarded. Recently, Sara has begun to think that only Mihi understands the hard work that goes into her proposals.

Mihi loves her job. It is fun being with her friends, and she knows she can make sense out of whatever they come up with. She worries a little about the company's lack of direction and wants them all to see the same big picture that she does, but Mihi knows they will come around if she plans carefully enough. Although she doesn't know what to do about Sara, Mihi is convinced that she can figure out a way for the company to work, no matter what. When Sara first spoke to her about her problem communicating long distance, Mihi went online and ordered several books about conflict and communication. She plans to speak privately with each partner over the next few weeks so that they can develop a master plan.

☙

Small Group Discussion: We all have ways of learning that have worked best for us. Your approach to learning and to communicating information has been developed over a period of years. Usually, we each end up with an approach that works for us, one that we have been rewarded for in some way.

Our individual approaches to learning are not set in stone—far from it. Having an idea of how we learn and teach and whether it works for the people we need to communicate with is a good first step to adjusting our style so that it works in a specific situation or with a specific person.

Ask one another: "What should Art, Margaret, Mihi, and Sara do now?"

Talk to the people in your group about whom they are most like—Art, Margaret, Mihi, or Sara? (You can probably answer "a little of each," but for the sake of the exercise, pick the person whose preferences are closest to yours. There is no right answer or one best preference.)

Whom are you most like?

Whom are you least like?

THE SHARED RESOURCE

When we think of conflict as a win/lose situation, we have only one of three possible outcomes: win, lose, or draw. When we think of it as a win/win situation, we have to use different strategies: make it even, make it bigger, or make it different.

Here is what I mean by make it even. We can both win if we are fighting about something that can be split down the middle, or otherwise divided in a way that makes everyone happy.

Let us say there is a worker whose salary is split between two departments. The head of one department uses two-thirds of the worker's time, and the other is angry because she only gets one-third of the worker's time but pays for half. How can they make this even?

Regulate the worker's hours to ensure that the time is split 50/50.

Change the percentage paid by each to accurately reflect the allocation of the worker's time.

Charge each department according to the hours actually worked in each department.

Etc.

MY DAD AND THE LAST BROWNIE

I grew up in the middle of a family of six kids. I don't think we gave our parents too much grief, but with eight people in the house, there were naturally things to disagree about.

We all know the classic complaint of children to a parent, "He's looking at me!" When I was about five years old, my older brother actually complained to our mother that I was not only looking at him, but that I was looking at his food. Hard not to with six kids—the oldest was age nine, the youngest age one—crammed around the kitchen table.

Needless to say, Mom became adept at knowing who got which color drinking glass, whose turn it "really" was to do dishes, and any number of other crucial decisions. She had the answer to all of these judicial questions, but for some reason, it was my father who ruled on cases where there was no clear precedent.

Somewhere along the line, Dad picked up an interesting even-steven solution for the problem of two kids and one last brownie. "Here," he said, giving the knife to my brother, "You cut the brownie in half." Then he looked at me, "You get to pick who gets which half."

You never saw such careful cutting in your life. Both kids became involved in solving the problem of being certain that the solution was even-steven.

And Dad was off the hook.

RUEBEN AND LAUREL

Two managers, Rueben and Laurel, have worked together for five years and have become good friends. Rueben is a top salesperson and Laurel heads up the company's customer service unit. They often drop into one another's offices to talk over problems. Both of them look forward to working on projects together and tend to agree about what to do in various business situations. Although they don't generally socialize outside of the office, they have met one another's spouses at company functions and always talk about getting everybody together for dinner some weekend. They consider themselves friends and allies.

In a corporate consolidation, the two managers' departments have been merged, and Laurel has been put in charge. Rueben now reports to her. Laurel has been told to move out of her office and into what used to be Rueben's area.

There is only one office, and Laurel needs it. Rueben will have to move into a cubicle.

Rueben's main function is sales. He cannot see how he can possibly do a good job from a cubicle. He has carefully set up his office to impress the clients who come in to meet him. It is decorated with sales and golfing awards, and the shelves are full of customer mementos and thank-you gifts.

Laurel has always worked in customer service. She works with most of her customers on the telephone. Her old office was decorated simply: a white-board, a few telephone books, and several filing cabinets for customer records. Laurel needs to work in a quiet environment. She also needs a private place where she can meet with her employees, and a secure place for confidential files. Besides, she is now the director of the newly formed department, and she feels it would send the wrong message if she were working in a cubicle while one of her male subordinates had a nice office.

❧

Discussion:
What can Laurel and Rueben do to "make it bigger"?

Hint: Look at what they both need, redefine the problem, and go from there. Remember that how well your solution works will depend largely upon how Laurel and Rueben feel about it.

TWO SISTERS, ONE ORANGE

In the early 1900s, Mary Parker Follett studied and wrote about conflict and how people could work things out to benefit everyone involved. Follett told this story to explain one approach to conflict.

There were two sisters who both wanted the only orange in the house. As they argued about it, their mother came in and suggested that they cut it in half. They both refused this compromise, so the mother asked them what they needed the orange for. One sister needed the orange to make juice, and half an orange was hardly enough. The other needed the orange for a cake she was baking and needed the entire peel.

Of course, the clever mother helped the two daughters see that they could both be satisfied. One got the peel, the other got the fruit.

Now some hard work for you. Talk to the others in your group and come up with some other situations—from life, from work, from the news, whatever—where things worked out or could work out the same way as Mary Parker Follett's story of the two sisters and the one orange. If you know of a folktale or a story from your childhood that teaches a similar lesson, share that as well.

THE LEAF BLOWER

John Pritchett lives alone in the house his parents bought when he was eight years old. John is now eighty-three. He does not go out as often as he used to, but he still enjoys sitting on the porch on a summer evening and watching the neighborhood kids play ball or tag in the street in front of his house. His next-door neighbors, the Junos, moved in about a year and a half ago.

Fred and Patricia Juno bought their house using cash from a wedding present as a large part of their down payment. The house was a fixer-upper when they got it, and they have done most of their own work to get the house the way they want it. Fred spends a great deal of time on his yard. The small front lawn is a manicured carpet of deep green. A white wrought-iron bench encircles an old chestnut tree that shelters the front porch.

John used to chat with the Junos from his front porch, and even lent them tools when they first started their restoration project. He started complaining, however, when they bought a gas-powered leaf blower.

"Makes a lot of noise and more mess than it cleans up," said John. "The same amount of time with a broom and some common courtesy is all you need."

In the autumn, the Junos's chestnut tree drops leaves on the ground, as do many of the other old trees that line the street. John Pritchett has been complaining lately that the Junos's leaves are in his yard and on his driveway. John has even called the police twice telling them that Fred and Patricia are littering in his yard. He says that they intentionally blow the leaves from their yard into his with the leaf blower. The police came out both times but told John there was nothing they could do.

John put a letter in the Junos's mailbox. He called them names in the letter and said that the neighborhood was a good neighborhood before they came in and that they had better watch their step or they would be sorry.

Last Saturday, Patricia took a plate of cookies over to John as a peace offering. John cursed at her through his closed screen door and told her if she didn't get off the porch he would shoot her. Patricia went home and told Fred.

Fred had had about enough of this. He took his cordless telephone out of the house and onto John's front lawn. He waved the telephone at the window and shouted, "I'm calling the cops, you crazy SOB!"

At that moment, John's son Mike drove up with his family. Mike told Fred to get off his father's property. John shouted from the house that he had a gun and was willing to use it.

"So do I, old man," yelled Fred and pulled a small revolver from his waistband. Mike ran back to his car and reached into the glove box for his cell phone. Fred thought Mike was reaching for a gun.

Debriefing
Ask the group:

What do you think happened next?

Why do you think that would be how this story would end?

PART FOUR

TOOLBOX

This section contains the outline for the full two-day workshop as well as recommendations for a one-day and three half-day workshops. You will also find information about additional resources that will give you background in approaches to conflict and systems thinking, and on facilitating collaborative workshops. Flip charts used in the workshop are reproduced in this section.

WORKSHOP INFORMATION

OUTLINE FOR FULL TWO-DAY WORKSHOP

Day One

9:00–9:10   Introduction to the Workshop (10 minutes)

Module 1. Awareness

9:10–9:15   Introduction and Objectives (5 minutes)

9:15–9:20   *The Bell Curve* (5 minutes)

9:20–10:00   *Naming the Workshop* (40 minutes)
         Brainstorming
           Discussion
           Voting
           Building Consensus

10:00–10:15   Break

10:15–10:35   Ways of Seeing (20 minutes)
         Introduction
         Story and Discussion: *To Bag or Not to Bag, Good Manners,* and *The Lilliputian Egg Wars*

10:35–10:45   Ways of Knowing (10 minutes)
         The Second Look
         Story and Discussion: *The Farmer on the Porch, The Pink Moment, The Colored Ball,* and *The Blind Men and the Elephant*

10:45–11:00   Ways of Learning (15 minutes)
         Losing Sara

11:00–11:15   Break

11:15–11:40   Ways of Living (25 minutes)
         Do the Right Thing

11:40–12:30   Ways of Seeing Conflict (50 minutes)
         Win, Lose, or Draw
         Make It Even, Make It Bigger, or Make It Different
           Make It Even
           Make It Bigger
           Make It Different
         The Shared Resource

My Dad and the Last Brownie
Two Sisters, One Orange
Reflection: *What Do I Think About Conflict Right Now?*

12:30–1:30   Lunch

Module 2. Response

1:30–1:40   Introduction and Objectives (10 minutes)
1:40–2:20   Reflection: *"Good" Conflict?* (40 minutes)
2:20–2:35   Break
2:35–3:35   *Party Time* (1 hour)
3:35–3:50   Break
3:50–4:05   Reflection: *How Can This Possibly Be Good for Me?* (15 minutes)
4:05–4:20   Wrap Up Day One (15 minutes)

Day Two

9:00–9:10   Review of Day One (10 minutes)

Module 3. Actions

9:10–9:15   Introduction and Objectives (5 minutes)
9:15–9:25   Conflict Intervention (10 minutes)

Solving Problems

9:25–9:30   Introduction (5 minutes)
9:30–9:35   *Two Siblings and One Orange—Take One* (5 minutes)
9:35–12:30   Practice Mediation (2 hours, 55 minutes)
                       Looking Neutral
12:30–1:30   Lunch

Transformation

1:30–1:40   Introduction (10 minutes)
1:40–1:45   *Two Siblings and One Orange—Take Two* (5 minutes)
1:45–2:15   How Deep Is Too Deep? (30 minutes)
2:15–2:30   Break

My Personal Conflict Strategy

2:30–2:31   Introduction (1 minute)
2:31–3:15   Choosing Thoughts (44 minutes)
3:15–3:30   Choosing Words (15 minutes)

3:30–3:45	Break
3:45–4:20	Choosing Actions (35 minutes)
4:20–4:35	Break
4:35–5:05	Our Group Conflict Strategy (30 minutes)
5:05–5:20	Close (15 minutes) Check-in: Does our name for conflict still work? Individual objectives check Evaluation

OUTLINE FOR ONE-DAY WORKSHOP

This shortened version of the workshop leaves out the group approaches to conflict; however, it provides a good opportunity for individual reflection and learning.

8:00–8:05	Introduction (5 minutes)
8:05–8:10	*The Bell Curve* (5 minutes)

8:10–8:30	Ways of Seeing (20 minutes)
	    Introduction
	    Story and Discussion

8:30–8:40	Ways of Knowing (10 minutes)
	    Truth
	    The Second Look
	    The Blind Men and the Elephant

8:40–8:55	Ways of Learning (15 minutes) *Losing Sara*
8:55–9:20	Ways of Living (25 minutes) *Do the Right Thing*

9:20–10:10	Ways of Seeing Conflict (50 minutes)
	    Win, Lose, or Draw
	    Make It Even, Make It Bigger, or Make It Different
	        Make It Even
	        Make It Bigger
	        Make It Different
	    Two Sisters, One Orange
	    Reflection: *What Do I Think About Conflict Right Now?*

10:10–10:25	Break

Response

10:25–11:00	Reflection: *"Good" Conflict?* (35 minutes)
11:00–11:10	Conflict Intervention (10 minutes)
11:10–11:15	*Two Siblings and One Orange—Take One* (5 minutes)
11:15–12:15	Lunch
12:15–3:00	Practice Mediation (2 hours, 45 minutes) *Looking Neutral*
3:00–3:15	Break
3:15–3:20	*Two Siblings and One Orange—Take Two* (5 minutes)

My Personal Conflict Strategy

3:20–3:21	Introduction (1 minute)
3:21–4:00	Choosing Thoughts (39 minutes)
4:00–4:15	Choosing Words (15 minutes)
4:15–4:45	Choosing Actions (30 minutes)
4:45–4:55	Close (10 minutes)

OUTLINE FOR HALF-DAY WORKSHOP: MEDIATION PRACTICE

This workshop stresses mediation skills. It is most effective with a small group of no more than ten people so that each participant gets at least two opportunities to practice mediating. The better the feedback from those practicing, the more successful the workshop will be.

8:00–8:05	Introduction (5 minutes)
8:05–8:10	*The Bell Curve* (5 minutes)
8:10–9:00	Ways of Seeing Conflict (50 minutes)
	Win, Lose, or Draw
	Make It Even, Make It Bigger, or Make It Different
	Make It Even
	Make It Bigger
	Make It Different
	Two Sisters, One Orange
	Reflection: *What Do I Think About Conflict Right Now?*
9:00–9:05	*Two Siblings and One Orange—Take One* (5 minutes)
9:05–12:00	Practice Mediation (2 hours, 55 minutes)
	Looking Neutral
12:00–12:15	Break
12:15–12:20	*Two Siblings and One Orange—Take Two* (5 minutes)
12:20–12:30	Close (10 minutes)

OUTLINE FOR HALF-DAY WORKSHOP: CONFLICT AWARENESS

The first half of day one in the two-day workshop can stand alone in helping people to begin examining their points of view about conflict.

9:00–9:05	Introduction and Objectives (5 minutes)
9:05–9:10	*The Bell Curve* (5 minutes)
9:10–9:50	*Naming the Workshop* (40 minutes)
	Brainstorming
	Discussion
	Voting
	Building Consensus
9:50–10:10	Ways of Seeing (20 minutes)
	Introduction
	Story and Discussion
10:10–10:25	Break
10:25–10:35	Ways of Knowing (10 minutes)
	Truth
	The Second Look
	The Blind Men and the Elephant
10:35–10:50	Ways of Learning (15 minutes)
	Losing Sara
10:50–11:05	Break
11:05–11:30	Ways of Living (25 minutes)
	Do the Right Thing
11:30–12:20	Ways of Seeing Conflict (50 minutes)
	Win, Lose, or Draw
	Make It Even, Make It Bigger, or Make It Different
	Make It Even
	Make It Bigger
	Make It Different
	Two Sisters, One Orange
	Reflection: *What Do I Think About Conflict Right Now?*
12:20–12:30	Close (10 minutes)

OUTLINE FOR HALF-DAY WORKSHOP: RESPONSES TO CONFLICT

With some modifications, the response section can stand alone as a half-day workshop. The emphasis is on making choices about how to respond in conflict situations.

8:00–8:05	Introduction (5 minutes)
8:05–8:10	*The Bell Curve* (5 minutes)
8:10–8:30	Ways of Seeing (20 minutes) 　　Introduction 　　Story and Discussion
8:30–8:40	Ways of Knowing (10 minutes) 　　Truth 　　The Second Look 　　*The Blind Men and the Elephant*
8:40–9:05	Ways of Living (25 minutes) 　　*Do the Right Thing*
9:05–9:55	Ways of Seeing Conflict (50 minutes) 　　Win, Lose, or Draw 　　Make It Even, Make It Bigger, or Make It Different 　　　　Make It Even 　　　　Make It Bigger 　　　　Make It Different
9:55–10:10	Break
10:10–10:50	Reflection: *"Good" Conflict?* (40 minutes)
10:50–10:55	Reflection: *How Can This Possibly Be Good for Me?* (5 minutes)

My Personal Conflict Strategy

10:55–10:56	Introduction (1 minute)
10:56–11:40	Choosing Thoughts (44 minutes)
11:40–11:55	Choosing Words (15 minutes)
11:55–12:20	Choosing Actions (25 minutes)
12:20–12:30	Close (10 minutes)

Additional Resources

LEARNING

Preparing for Peace: Conflict Transformation Across Cultures by John Paul Lederach (Syracuse, NY: Syracuse University Press, 1995). John Paul Lederach writes about his international experiences and outlines key concepts for creating training content along with workshop participants.

Journal of Accelerated Learning and Teaching can be found online at www.ialearn.org. The journal features articles about training and educational techniques that engage the learner emotionally for high-impact learning.

The *Learning Style Inventory* is a simple, but very helpful, instrument that can be used to help individuals and groups learn how to adjust their behavior to allow for differing information-processing preferences. For copies of the *LSI*, and for an easy-to-follow facilitation guide, contact McBer & Company at 800-729-8074.

Group Techniques for Idea Building by Carl M. Moore (Thousand Oaks, CA: Sage, 1994). A basic overview of proven techniques for brainstorming and building group consensus.

CONFLICT

The Mediator's Handbook by Jennifer E. Beer with Eileen Stief (Gabriola Island, BC, Canada: New Society, 1997) goes into great detail for people who want to learn more about how to mediate disputes between two parties.

The Promise of Mediation: Responding to Conflict Through Empowerment and Recognition by Robert A. Baruch Bush and Joseph P. Folger (San Francisco: Jossey-Bass, 1994) is the definitive guide to helping people in conflict acknowledge their own abilities while recognizing the value of the other person.

Aikido has been called the peaceful martial art. If you are interested in learning more about how calming your mind and body can help you find your own constructive approaches to conflict, visit www.well.com/~dooley/Aikido. This Web site provides stories and exercises as well as links to a handful of respected Aikido and other practitioners interested in organizational issues.

Getting Past No: Negotiating Your Way from Confrontation to Cooperation by William Ury (New York: Bantam Books, 1993). This is not only the book that advises you to go to the balcony, but is a clear, concise guide for people who want to successfully negotiate conflicts in a way that leaves everyone standing at the end.

Tom Peters needs little introduction. His classic best-selling books on innovative management rarely address conflict specifically, but Peters in person is conflict personified. If you have the opportunity and can afford the often high-priced ticket, go see Tom Peters speak. He is purposely outrageous, and a living demonstration that conflict can be the best way to discover new ways of seeing the world. As he has said in his seminar: "When two people in business always agree, one of them is unnecessary."

Resolving Identity-Based Conflict in Nations, Organizations, and Communities by Jay Rothman (San Francisco: Jossey-Bass, 1997). Rothman draws upon his experience as a consultant, teacher, and peacemaker in Israel to explain an approach to resolving entrenched conflicts that are outgrowths of the identities of the participants.

Dr. Seuss is right at home with all of these other doctors when it comes to explaining the dynamics of conflict and how it can escalate. The good doctor's *The Butter Battle Book* (New York: Random House, 1984) is not only a favorite of my editor's four-year-old, but a good reminder to all of us that it can be useful to trace deep-seated, seemingly intractable conflicts back to their origins.

SYSTEMS THINKING AND DIALOGUE

The Fifth Discipline: The Art & Practice of the Learning Organization by Peter M. Senge (New York: Doubleday, 1990). If you are planning an organizational strategy for dealing with conflict, read *The Fifth Discipline* before you read anything else. Like many books about organizations, there is little mention of interpersonal differences, but there is true power in Senge's understanding and explanation of the systems we design for work, their impact on our behavior, and how we can go about changing them.

The Fifth Discipline Fieldbook: Strategies and Tools for Building a Learning Organization by Peter M. Senge, Art Kleiner, Charlotte Roberts, Richard B. Ross, and Bryan J. Smith (New York: Doubleday, 1994). This collection of articles is a valuable how-to for creating a team or organizational environment that allows the safe, open exchange of differing ideas. Of particular interest to facilitators of the workshop in this book is an article by Rick Ross explaining the "ladder of inference" and another by Ross and Art Kleiner that teaches the "left-hand column" exercise. Both are stimulating ways for helping people to identify the way they choose their words, actions, and points of view.

Flip Charts

The Conflict Management Skills Workshop

Two Ways of Seeing Conflict

1. *A Contest:*
   - *Win*
   - *Lose*
   - *Draw*

2. *A Problem to Solve Together:*
   - *Make It Even*
   - *Make It Bigger*
   - *Make It Different*

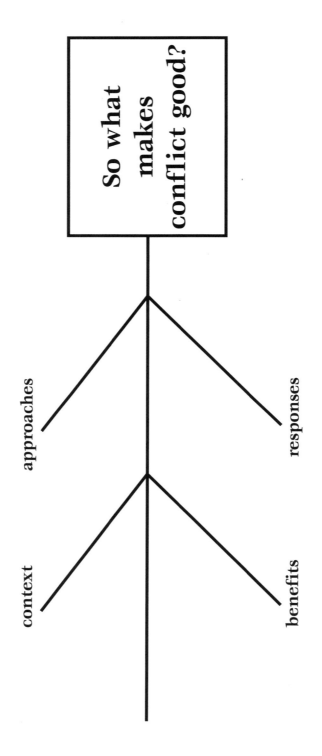

So what
makes
conflict good?

approaches

responses

context

benefits

Party-Time Rules of Engagement

1. Opening Statement (2 min.)

2. Questions from the Floor (3 min.)

3. Closing statement (2 min.)

Mediation Practice Schedule

1. Prep: Select case, select roles, read case.   (3–5 min.)

2. Mediator: Greet participants.

3. Mediator: Introduce the process: (2–3 min.)

    a. Confidentiality

    b. "Looking neutral"

    c. Walk-through of the process

4. Take turns.   (5 min. for each participant)

5. Exchange openly.   (5–7 min.)

6. Identify solutions.   (5–7 min.)

7. Mediator: Write agreement.   (3–5 min.)

8. Mediator: Thank/praise the participants.

9. Debrief as a group.   (5–10 min.)

10. Begin again with new mediator.

How Deep Is Too Deep?

	Too Deep	About Right	Not Deep Enough
1. Help communicate better.			
2. Solve the problem and move on.			
3. Help learn about respect.			
4. Help with contributing feelings.			
5. Help with conflicting beliefs.			
6. Help understand cultural differences.			
7. Help people see response patterns.			

continued

	Too Deep	About Right	Not Deep Enough
8. Help people to see others' points of view.			
9. Help people choose words.			
10. Balance power.			
11. Coach better listening.			
12. Help acknowledge others' needs.			
13. Help find common ground.			
14. Let people be upset.			
15. Help people change the system.			

continued

	Too Deep	About Right	Not Deep Enough
16. Let people not fix it.			
17. Be sure they talk about real issues.			
18. Stick up for the underdog.			
19. Make experts.			
20. Stop lawsuits.			
21. Settle once and for all.			
22. Convert.			

Nontoxic Language

You are lazy.	Help me understand how you choose what is important enough to do.
I hate you.	This makes me angry.
That was stupid.	I don't understand that.
You're a liar.	Our facts don't agree.
You have a big mouth.	

How Should We Do This?

Action:

Who:

When:

Completion
Criteria:

INDEX